“Early Christianity is marked by the good, And people almost never simply fall into reflect a mixture of the three. While many Christian treatments of church history tend to emphasize our ‘greatest hits’ and reflect a tinge of triumphalism, Derek Cooper’s *Sinners and Saints* recognizes the importance of being ruthlessly honest about our past. Such honesty is essential to understanding how God has worked through flawed humans in the past as well as in the present. This *Real Story of Early Christianity* is a page-turner that recognizes that authenticity in our present Christian witness begins with our willingness to tell the truth about our past. This way of telling our story is honest, compelling, and edifying!”

—Roy E. Ciampa,
Nida Institute for Biblical Scholarship

“Derek Cooper has written a vibrant and energetic account of church history that usually gets forgotten or covered up. He offers no romantic narration of the good old days; instead Cooper lays out many of the absurd, embarrassing, funny, scary, and plain weird things that happened in the early church. You could just as well call it the ‘horrible history of the early church’ or ‘the underbelly of church history.’ It will make you laugh, squirm, raise your eyebrows in confusion, and even gross you out. A truly unique entrée into early church history!”

—Dr. Michael F. Bird,
Lecturer in Theology at Ridley College, Melbourne, Australia

“Virtually every family has an ‘interesting’ past—and the family of God is no different. Derek Cooper uses his skillful mastery of church history to shine a candid yet hope-filled light on the church, helping us catch glimpses of our brothers and sisters with their makeup off. If you want to know what the church’s past is *really* like—free from cynicism and dry academic writing—this book is for you.”

—J.R. Briggs,
founder of Kairos Partnerships,
author of *Fail: Finding Hope and Grace in the Midst of Ministry Failure*

“In *Sinners and Saints*, Derek Cooper escorts the reader on a revealing journey through early church history. Lovers of history and those who find history boring will enjoy and learn alike from this engaging book. It also provides a much needed corrective for Christians inclined to idealize and idolize Christian leaders in the past, as well as Christian leaders today—all who are without exception both sinners and saints.”

—Carolyn Custis James,
author of *Malestrom: Manhood Swept into the Currents of a Changing World*
and *Finding God in the Margins: The Book of Ruth*

"Few books these days surprise me, but Derek Cooper's *Sinners and Saints* has done just that. At times slapstick funny, at times borderline inappropriate, and at times profoundly moving, this book turns the black-and-white version of the church's history into living color. As a lifelong reader of early church history, I learned new things on every page—things I had never read or heard before about the church I love so much. It is clear from this powerful book that Derek Cooper loves the church, the same church our Lord loves and gave his life for."

—The Rev. David W. Peters,
author of P*ost-Traumatic God: How the Church Cares for People Who Have Been to Hell and Back*

"Finally, a book about Christian history that does not pull any punches. Many tend to view the early church through rose colored glasses, as a glorious time we should all strive to return to. Cooper's brutally honest portrayal of early Christianity and the surrounding culture reminds the church that we are just as fragile today as the earliest Christians were centuries ago and that there is no shame in being human. Cooper presents a thorough, detailed, user-friendly, and often gritty account of early Christianity that is both highly readable and absolutely fascinating."

—Bill Curtis,
President of Christian History Institute

REAL CHURCH HISTORY

SINNERS AND SAINTS

The Real Story of Early Christianity

Derek Cooper

Sinners and Saints: The Real Story of Early Christianity

Published by Kregel Publications, a division of Kregel Inc., 2450 Oak Industrial Dr. NE, Grand Rapids, MI 49505-6020.

ISBN 978-0-8254-4407-4

Printed in the United States of America

18 19 20 21 22 / 5 4 3 2 1

THIS BOOK IS WARMLY DEDICATED
TO FRANK JAMES III,
WHO HAS ALWAYS ENCOURAGED
ME TO TELL THE TRUTH.

CONTENTS

ACKNOWLEDGMENTS

I would like to thank the fine team at Kregel Publications for their work on our series *Sinners and Saints: The Real Story of Christianity*, beginning with this first volume. It is always a pleasure to speak with Herb Bateman, and more so to hear his belly laugh. Dennis Hillman and Paul Hillman pushed me to write a better manuscript. Laura Bartlett and Shawn Vander Lugt were very helpful in the latter stages of the book. Thanks to all of you.

I'm also grateful for colleagues of mine who read specific chapters and offered insight. This illustrious list includes J. R. Briggs, Barb Cooper, Jason Craig, Ed Cyzewski, Pete Enns, Cliff Gehret, Joe Hackman, Sandy Haney, Carolyn Custis James, Frank James, Nijay Gupta, Daniel Kirk, Rick Miller, Cyndi Parker, David Peters, and David Peters (yes, I have two friends with the same name who both read portions of this book). I'm deeply appreciative of your time, perspectives, and feedback.

In addition, I commend Jason Craig for suggesting an alternate title for the book, which, for the sake of public decency, will not be repeated here. I give a right-hand victorious salute to Cliff Gehret for encouraging me to sound more like Joel Osteen. I acknowledge Cyndi Parker for motivating me to remove more sarcasm than I should have. I applaud Denise Baum for her indefatigable zeal when processing interlibrary loans, which may or may not have been accompanied by raised eyebrows and disapproving glances at some of my more dubious book selections. I recognize Paul Hillman for urging me to delete one of the most depressing introductions to a book since Sylvia Plath. I extol Frank James for reading every word of the manuscript—at least that's what he told me. Finally, I thank the church for giving me more delightfully temperamental characters than a Hollywood screenplay. Apart from one or two of you, the rest of you lot have a lot of explaining to do.

Introduction

GETTING REAL WITH CHRISTIANITY'S PAST

If the church were a celebrity, it would have a serious public relations problem. Here are the headlines. Yesterday a prominent pastor was caught having an affair. Today an entire church board was charged with tax evasion. Tomorrow a celebrated Christian leader will be fired for racist comments. Although the church has certainly had its share of inspirational figures, ethical victories, and heroic achievements, such have often been overshadowed by unsavory characters, moral failures, and embarrassing escapades.

Despite our awareness of the church's declining public appeal today, however, many good-natured Christians are completely unfamiliar with our sinful past. We may reluctantly acknowledge the shortcomings of our most popular leaders and even confess the private sins of our own hearts, but we are not accustomed to calling into question the motives of Jesus's disciples or of interrogating our most famous forebears. To the contrary, many pious believers look back with twinkles in our eyes to the "golden age" of the early church when no one faced a hint of conflict, no one lacked food or shelter, and no one suffered from morning breath.

Lite-Brite. Courtesy of Dhscommtech.

Though unintentional, part of our starry-eyed nostalgia for the past comes from an uncritical understanding of the Bible. As I often joke with my students, reading Scripture is like using the toy Lite-Brite. Depending on the template used, most any design can be made. We assume that there is only one template in the toy box, but there are actually any number of ways to make a design. For far too long we have unconsciously used the following set of verses as our sole template of the ancient church:

> All the believers were one in heart and mind. No one claimed that any of his possessions was his own, but they shared everything they had...There were no needy persons among them. For from time to time those who owned lands or houses sold them, brought the money from the sales and put it at the apostles' feed, and it was distributed to anyone as he had need. (Acts 4:32, 34–35)

If these were the only kinds of verses in the New Testament describing early Christianity, there would be nothing left to do other than complete our sublime design, turn off the lights, and stand in awe of our wonderful creation. To be completely honest, I wish things really were this simple and straightforward. However, we need not venture more than five verses from this idyllic template before we witness Ananias and Sapphira, presumably filled with the same Holy Spirit poured on all the believers in Acts 2, committing "fraud" (5:2) by lying about the land they donated to the apostles and suffering a most abrupt and shocking demise as a result—death by the Holy Spirit.

The story of Ananias and Sapphira is a story we don't like, but that doesn't mean we can ignore it. Despite the consternation it causes us, it balances out the better known and more benevolent retellings that Christians prefer to ponder. For as we continue to insert our plastic pegs into the black box, a more symmetrical reading of Scripture can't help but notice the heartbreaking conflicts, the questionable conduct, and the sinful actions that constantly dot our design. Whether the "sharp disagreement" (Acts 15:39) between Barnabas and Paul about whether to bring along John Mark on their missionary journeys, whether Peter and Paul's infamous quarrel about how to minister to the Gentiles (Gal. 2:11–14), whether Demas's desertion of Paul because Demas "loved this world" (2 Tim. 4:10), or whether the Apostle John's public denunciation of Diotrephes for

***The Death of Ananias* by Raphael.**

advancing "malicious nonsense" (3 John 1:10), the church is more human, and occasionally less humane, than we care to recognize or admit. Christians who do not understand this important truth run the risk of harm by not guarding our hearts against the inevitable sinfulness that resides in the core of humanity. For although we, the church, like to think of ourselves as "in" the world but not "of" it, we have to recognize that our heavenly spirits are still yoked to our earthly bodies.

But before we paint the picture of early Christians with too dark a brush, I hasten to add that the first Christians were not wholly bad or evil. Not in the least. On the contrary, the church was, and is, as Paul wrote to the Ephesians, "God's handiwork" (Eph. 2:10), a masterpiece of the ages, to be marveled out and appreciated by onlookers of all backgrounds and temperaments. The church is a splendid masterwork, one painted in many beautiful hues and shades. It is beautiful and pleasing in God's sight and surely the object of his affection. But it's not flawless. The church, as holy and Spirit-filled as it is, will remain all too human while men and women and boys and girls dwell in this fallen world. It does the church no good to pretend that we are something that we are not—and we are neither individually impeccable nor collectively exemplary. Nor does it do the world any good to imagine that our history is nothing but admirable despite the fact that the repulsive exploits of some of our most celebrated church leaders are regularly paraded about in news reports and on social media.

WHY I AM WRITING THIS BOOK

Although unconventional, in the pages that follow I seek to offer a more balanced picture of early Christianity as a way to both strengthen the body of Christ and to offer an authentic witness to the world. Please let me explain. When I was in seminary, the most difficult class I took was not Advanced Hebrew, not Advanced Greek, nor even one curiously titled "Q"—an entire class, believe it or not, dedicated to a hypothetical document that has never been found and which many scholars believe never existed. Instead, the most difficult class I took was one innocuously entitled "Introduction to Evangelism." In addition to the requirement of sharing my faith with thirteen different people over the course of a semester, I had to complete an "evangelistic project" that required me to survey dozens of non-Christians in my hometown. In the project, the survey question I remember most vividly asked non-Christians why they were not Christians—a pointed question if there ever was one. The majority of respondents said something to this effect: "I am not a Christian because Christians are hypocrites who cover up their past." Among the examples cited were the Crusades, witch hunts, intellectual battles against science, support of slavery, systemic racism, justification of war, subjugation of women, collusion with the state, pedophilia, and anti-Semitism.

As a church historian and committed Christian, this resounding response along with its tangible examples is a bitter pill that I am still attempting to swallow. And, unfortunately, rather than being a minority report, recent surveys corroborate my findings. According to *unChristian*, among many other sources, younger generations believe that *Christianity* and *hypocrisy* are synonymous terms.[1] It grieves me to read these surveys. I only wish everyone knew, as I do as a church historian, how much the church has blessed the world in its 2000 years of existence. It is Christians, after all, who have been at the forefront of founding hospitals, funding health clinics, starting schools, rescuing the abused, caring for the elderly, rehabilitating the imprisoned, sheltering the homeless, strengthening the family, offering mental health services, providing spiritual guidance, and generally improving society. The stories of Christians standing up for justice and serving those in need are too many to mention. In fact, despite what I will do in this book, I could go on singing the praises of the church page after page. But to what avail? Why contribute more white noise to the clamor?

Part of the reason why so many non-Christians believe that Christianity is nothing but one long reign of terror is because all they hear us talk about is our triumphs, but never our defeats. Within a society that so highly values transparency, honesty, and authenticity, our reluctance to address the foibles of our fathers confirms a mounting suspicion in the minds of many that we have precious little to offer people living today. Given our current social climate, and all the undeniable scandals in which the church has been variously implicated, how can we continue to idealize biblical characters, glamorize the early years of the church, and sentimentalize our origins? Perhaps there is a better way to live in a post-Christian world; a better way to bend towards heaven while keeping our feet firmly planted in the mud; a better way to tell our story.

In this book, let's trod a different path. Unlike countless other church history books that dance around the distasteful details of our Christian past, let's humanize our history. Counterintuitively perhaps, let's emphasize as much grit as glory, let's feature as much flesh as faith, and let's showcase as many sinners as saints. It's important for you to know at the onset, however, that we are not going to do this because we think mudslinging is a spiritual discipline, but only because we believe truth-telling is. I, personally, have no desire to sully the reputation of saints, nor do I find any pleasure in wallowing in the faults of our most faithful. When I air the dirty laundry of our most hallowed heroes and heroines, I am fully aware of all the clean clothes they have neatly pressed and attractively arrayed in their dresser drawers. Because of the nature of this book, I will not usually refer to that clean laundry; but make no mistake: I know that it's there.

In short, I am imploring you, the reader, not to confuse my intention to offer a candid history of early Christianity with your impression that I have an axe to grind with the body of Christ. Nothing could be further from the truth. Truth is, my confidence in the body of believers to proclaim Christ's offer of salvation to the world does not waver, rankle, or panic just because Christians are humans who err rather than gods who do not. Nor am I dissuaded from the truth of Christianity because bushels of bad apples reside interspersed among orchards of healthy ones. We need not hire a search party to find the truth when it is staring us straight in the face: I am not writing this book because I am angry, bitter, or reactionary. I am simply writing it to correct the natural tendency of all people, Christians included, to cast our history in the best possible light. Although there's nothing wrong with highlighting our predecessors' sparks of sainthood, there is danger in failing to mention their flames of failure.

LETTING GO, LOOKING FOR GOD, AND LEANING IN

Because the path we are opting to take when discussing early Christianity is uncharted and unfamiliar, I am going to suggest we keep three concepts in mind while reading this book. These concepts will lead us into a deeper learning experience as we ponder the painfully honest history about to be presented, and they will also remind us that this book is designed to serve the body of Christ rather than to subvert it. After each chapter, I suggest that you spend a few minutes reflecting and praying. Commit to asking God, "What are you teaching me through this?" "What can I learn from the broken lives of the people discussed?" "How can I incorporate the truths of church history into my everyday life and that of my faith community?"

The first concept is called "Let go." All of us have preconceived ideas and biases. Like smudged contact lenses, these assumptions and biases color the interpretation of our environment, our social circles, and our reading of Scripture. They encourage us to see things from only our perspective, and we rarely discover how to remove the smudge so that we may see more clearly. As you read this book, pray that God will help you let go of your insistence that biblical figures and early Christian leaders have to be perfect. Instead, begin to recognize that early Christian leaders, like all our favorite characters in the Bible, were real people who mourned when experiencing loss, lashed out when

***Moses Breaking the Tablets of the Law* by Rembrandt.**

provoked, faltered when under temptation, and crumbled when undergoing persecution. Early Christian history is nothing if it is not a story of sinful saints who got angry like Moses, lied like Sarah, cheated like David, and drifted like Solomon. The stories of their lives are designed to push us closer to Christ our refuge, not give us a false sense of human greatness. Continually ask God, "What do I need to let go of in order to see this story anew?" "How can I read the Bible and the history of the church without needing to domesticate it?"

The second concept is called "Look for God." A raging fire may consume an entire block in a city. Life is taken, possessions are lost, and we mourn the destruction. But when the flames die out and we sift through the ashes, can we see where God resides in the ruin? As the apostle Paul famously declared, "when I am weak, then I am strong" (2 Cor. 12:10). Throughout the ages we see how God and flesh dance to different tunes but intersect at certain junctures. Can we see how God is at work in spite of sin? Can we celebrate and highlight human weakness in order to see God's strength? As the Bible makes clear, God has a reputation of liking messy people and messy things, and of allowing these to frame the beautiful backdrop to his dramatic plan of salvation. As Eugene Peterson poignantly put it, "the Word became flesh and blood, and moved into the neighborhood" (John 1:14, The Message). While in the neighborhood of Planet Earth, Christ, as Emmanuel or "God with us," was more than content to pitch his tent among the needy, among the desperate, and among the sinners. Recognizing that church history is simply a continuation of the drama of God's redemption from the Bible, we must not alter the structure of the last two acts in the play. As you reflect upon the strange union between God and flesh, continually be on the lookout for God by asking, "Where is God amidst the clutter?" "How does the weakness inherent in this person's life or in that situation's context illustrate God's strength?"

Finally, the third concept is called "Lean in." Lean into the lives of these misfits we know as Paul, Mary Magdalene, Tertullian, Origen, Constantine, and Augustine. They're our family, and every time we familiarize ourselves with their lives, we are transcending the sands of time and learning more about ourselves—our spiritual family. And just as we learn at a family reunion how to evade Cousin Johnny's crude jokes and why to avoid Aunt Miralda's tuna casserole, we also learn how to succeed in sports by watching Uncle Joe play intergenerational baseball and we learn how to cook delicious desserts by observing Grandfather Lewis make puff pastries and plumb pie.

As we learn from our spiritual godfathers and godmothers, uncles and aunts, grandparents and great grandparents, let them caution us as much as they encourage us. Let us learn from their vices as much as from their victories. And let us critique their lives as much as we celebrate them. For like us, they slipped, they stumbled, and they sinned. Though it times they seemed to transcend their human limitations, they never permanently surpassed their human flesh. They always remained as fragile as fine china. Nevertheless, God chose to use and work through them, just as he chooses to use and work through us. Studying their lives is our invitation to embrace our own imperfection. It is our invitation to acknowledge our brokenness. It is our invitation to be ourselves. If God uses these sinful saints, he can certainly use you, me, and many others. Let this truth bring you hope. As you attempt to lean into the lives of our ancient family members, consider asking God, "How can their lives encourage me or teach me?" "What can I learn from their stories about my own relationship with Christ?

STRUCTURE OF THE BOOK

To be sure, the forthright assessment of the church's past that we will present in this book will bruise our egos, but I believe that it will also give us hope for the future with the aim of making us more truthful and transparent reporters of the present. Christ, after all, has come to liberate us from idolatry, not to enslave us to fiction. The time has come for us to no longer overlook those parts of our past that are disgraceful to God and dishonoring to the world. The time has come for the church to give an honest evaluation of the good, the bad, and the ugly that we have done, beginning with the earliest Christians.

But how, exactly, are we supposed to candidly narrate a history that contains two millennia of skeletons in our church's closets? Rather than shining a light into the church's closet all at once, this initial volume illumines only the first five hundred years of Christianity's past. Additional volumes highlighting the remaining years of the church are to follow—skeletons and all. The ten chapters that comprise this volume proceed thematically rather than chronologically, meaning that every chapter stretches from the first to the sixth century. Though slightly different from the others, the first chapter sets the tone for the rest of the book. In short, as much as we envy the people living during the time of the Bible and during the first generation of the church, we really should not. It's not just that life spans were shorter and standards of living were inferior back then; the people were just as broken as we are today. Indeed, because we are so inclined to regard the early Christians as perpetually holier and happier than we are today, attention will be drawn to how challenging life in the past really was.

The remaining chapters will likewise provide a realistic depiction of early Christian living. In the following order, each of the major features of the early Christian experience will be put into perspective: leadership, martyrdom, worship, apologetics, heresy, scripture, money, sex, and missions. Though the aim of these chapters is certainly not to blacken the cloud of witnesses surrounding the church, we will candidly discuss early Christian leaders who sometimes put their own interests before that of the church's, martyrs who sometimes gave their lives for the wrong reasons, devotees who sometimes worshiped in bizarre ways, apologists who sometimes argued from poor and even racist logic, fundamentalists who sometimes bullied fellow Christians, believers who sometimes wanted to know more about their Savior than was for their own good, aristocrats who sometimes sought to buy their way into heaven, men who sometimes denigrated women and disdained sexual intercourse, and missionaries who sometimes spread the faith with mixed motives. If these Christians of yesteryear sound like those of today, it's because they are cut from the same cloth. It's because they are you, and it's because they are me. Let's see what their lives were *really* like.

ENDNOTES

1 David Kinnaman and Gabe Lyons, *unChristian: What a New Generation Really Thinks about Christianity...and Why It Matters* (Grand Rapids, MI: Baker, 2007), 41–60.

Chapter 1

LIVING IN THE REAL WORLD—DAILY LIFE

Despite dreamy landscapes cascading across contemporary Christmas Cards, there was nothing romantic about life in the ancient world. Life in the biblical past was laced with death, disease, and destitution. While best-selling American author Joel Osteen encourages us to "live our best life now," many ancient Christians were simply trying to survive. The average life expectancy, after all, was in the thirties, girls were married off to older men they scarcely knew and were likely pregnant by the age of thirteen, and they delivered their babies on dirt floors in their squalid one-room tenements. There were no systems of welfare to provide for the poor, no retirement homes to accommodate the elderly, and no way to post pictures online from one's vacation at the beach.

Truth is, the closer one gets to the "time of Jesus" or to the "age of the Bible," the closer one gets to malnutrition, persecution, privation, patriarchy, slavery, trauma, inequality, demonic possession, rampant poverty, and a lifetime of public toilets.[1] The apostle Paul captured the spirit of his age well when he wrote: "I desire to depart [from this world]" (Phil. 1:23). And there's little wonder why the last lines of the Bible are "Amen. Come, Lord Jesus" (Rev. 22:20).[2] The early Christians ached to be rid of the death-filled, heart-rending, and back-breaking world of the Bible.

> "Most persons [in the Roman Empire] lived miserable lives."[30]

YOUR WORST LIFE NOW

Because our tendency to romanticize the biblical and early Christian past is so rooted in our thinking, we are poised to resist this startling portrayal. We may think to ourselves, *Was life really* that *bad*? You tell me: How does it sound to be constantly battling tape worms, to be steadily suffering from malaria, or to be always wondering when your next meal would come? How does it sound to put your children to work before their tenth birthday, to be unable to read or write, or to have no way to advance your career? As much as we prefer this not to be true, such was life during the time of the Bible. Defying our expectations, archaeology has demonstrated that ancient people were routinely missing teeth, that they were not getting enough protein, and that delousing—as in the stripping of lice from one's hair with a comb—"may have been a daily routine for many people."[3]

Many of the things we take for granted in our convenience-laden lives were simply unattainable for most Christians: soap, sewage, dentistry, security, privacy, mobility, legal protection, pension, public education, electricity, kitchens, chimneys, even adequate access to food and water. And we can forget about paid vacation, emergency rooms, and three square meals a day. Bread, that high-carb temptation so often avoided by eaters today, was the staple of one's diet, while a good cut of beef was only available at the butcher's shop adjoining a pagan temple. Either way, according to historians, "The overwhelming majority of the population under Roman imperialism lived near the subsistence level."[4] This indicates that most Christians in the Roman Empire were just managing to scrounge up enough food each day to survive. Even among the house churches that Paul led in the homes of aristocratic Christians, it's likely that most of the saints assembled there "were poor, very poor, or desperately poor."[5]

"...the poor, a vast majority of the Roman population, were most vulnerable to food shortages and crises, and infectious diseases, and were subject to the shame, alienation, and the bias and indifference of the rich."[31]

AN URBAN AFFAIR

In addition to being paralyzed by poverty, early Christianity was also an utterly urban affair. Though most people in the ancient world lived in the countryside—naturally enough, as farming land was the only way to produce food—many early Christians still lived in the city. As one scholar explains, "peasants or country folk were not involved in the [Christian] movement until the late third or early fourth century."[6] This means that Christians today have to constantly resist the temptation to visualize a biblical spirituality of sheep grazing along a meadow. To the contrary, ancient Chris-

Public Bathroom in Ostia Antica, Italy. Courtesy of Fubar Obfusco.

Statue of Artemis. Courtesy of David Stanley.

tianity was lived out in the hustle and bustle of city life where prostitutes were for hire, pagan temples were on every street corner, and public gym classes were conducted in the nude. We might consider the destination of Paul's biblical letters in order to form a more historically accurate image: Rome, Corinth, Ephesus, Philippi, and Thessalonica were large, pagan, impoverished, and overcrowded cities. Ancient Rome, for instance, was more densely populated than modern Mumbai. Thus when Paul preached through this "Eternal City," we have to imagine his Roman toga caked in a crust of mud, trash, and excrement. As classical historian Mary Beard explains, Paul's Rome presented "squalid living conditions for most of the population."[7]

The cities in which Paul preached were also ones where odors assaulted one's sense of smell and sights arrested one's sense of decency. Paganism was evident on literally every street corner, and demonic possession was equally widespread. In such urban environments as the early Christian lived, whole families often lived in an unhygienic one-room tenement offering no heating, no running water, and no privacy. In the absence of public sanitation, many families defecated in pots that were tossed onto the street from an upstairs window. It was not at all uncommon for workers to live and labor in the same cramped space with other families. Some households even slept in shifts to accommodate all the people in the "crowded, poorly ventilated, and generally unhealthy conditions" in which so many Christians would have lived.[8] Because there was no space for a kitchen, and because cooking was a fire hazard among the island of poorly constructed apartments, most meals were eaten in the streets at the equivalent of fast-food joints called *popinae*

***Stele Licinia Amias Terme*. Courtesy of Marie-Lan Nguyen.**

in Latin or *thermopolia* in Greek. There were no sidewalks, no streetlamps, and no patrolmen.

Popina or Fast-food Restaurant in Pompeii. Courtesy of ell brown.

Raising a child in the ancient city was no walk in the park. Although the birth of a child today is often an occasion of celebration, it was a source of great anxiety in antiquity, even among wealthy families that could afford the best medical treatment. Countless children died every year from lack of basic medical care, and childbirth "was always the biggest killer of young adult women," "from senators' wives to slaves."[9] Tombstones of young children and their young mothers littered the Roman Empire, leaving us a trail of tears visible to this day. On one tombstone found in ancient Rome, the inscription of a deceased four-year old girl named Ampliata attempts to offer comfort to her bewailing mother: *Noli dolere, mamma, faciendum fuit*—"Don't be sad, mommy, it had to happen."[10]

Mummy Portrait of Deceased Girl. Courtesy of rob koopman.

In addition to constant exposure to death, children were likewise exposed to sex at a young age, as there was virtually no privacy among adults in their one-bedroom tenements. What's more, prostitution was not a private affair, roped off from the eyes of the innocent and carried out in a dark alley way. On the contrary, "it was a dominant institution, flourishing in the light of day."[11] Prostitution was state approved, modestly taxed, and socially acceptable. Back then, a hotel bill that included lodging, food, and sex was nothing out of the ordinary. Children were regularly exposed to nude statues and artwork forever garnering the streets, walls, and temples of every Roman city. And sexually explicit images cluttered walls and filled the minds of the young. Children would have been forced to begin work at a very young age, and very few of them would have received an education. Many children were also exposed (a common practice in the ancient world where children were left out in the elements), or sold into slavery. And at least half of all children did not even survive into adulthood.

IF I WERE A RICH MAN

If I have been painting the world of early Christianity with too dark and stark a brushstroke, that's because this realistic portrait is rarely acknowledged in churches, classrooms, and textbooks. It's certainly not true that all early Christians were like characters in the movie *Annie*, but they lived much poorer and more primitive lives than we want to admit. For the sake of argument, however, we can reconstruct what life would have been like for the fabulously wealthy. Rather than constituting the more than ninety-five percent of Roman inhabitants who worked like a dog just to make ends meet, here follows the life of a true blueblood aristocrat living among the top five percent of society. (Although there were some wealthy Christians in the church from the beginning, as even the New Testament indicates, their percentages were low until the third and fourth centuries.)

> To give a sense of the disparity of life in ancient Rome, historian Jerome Carcopino estimates that there was "only one private house [or *domus* in Latin] for every 26 blocks of apartment houses [or *insulae*]."[32]

As a Roman aristocrat, one's day generally revolved around bathing, eating, and accepting accolades. At some point in the day, after leading a prayer to the household gods and after receiving guests who are in his debt, a Roman *patronus* (patron) would swagger from his *domus* (large home) to the public bath house in his neatly pressed toga—clothing only allowed to be worn (of course, in a man-dominated world) by male Roman citizens. Several of his slaves and perhaps dozens of toadies, called "clients," would accompany him to demonstrate to everyone in the overcrowded streets just how important he was. (As strange as that sounds, this, in fact, was part of their duty as a "client.") At the public bathhouse, completely naked, the patron would lounge and converse with other rich people for hours as one of his slaves scrubbed his back with a shell while another guarded his clothing. In the afternoon, our *patronus* would return to his home, perhaps after a little time at the forum, for an elaborate meal in his *triclinium* (dining hall) with honored guests. The *triclinium* contained three couches that could accommodate up to nine people, who all lay down on their left elbows and ate with their right hands from a common dish in the middle of the room served by various slaves.

After dinner and over a glass of wine with his fellow aristocrats, the conversation might turn from gladiatorial races to the merits of religion. Because he would be an intimate acquaintance, and because it is well established that conversion largely took place in the ancient world (as today) through social networks, his friend lounging next to him may confide that he has recently become a Christian believer, and that he would like his friend to attend a worship service with him. The wealthy man might demur, but will consent after a few more drinks—it is Tuscan wine, after all. He eventually decides that the Christian life is for him, and seeks to learn what is required for what we call today "church membership." According to an early document called the *Apostolic Tradition*, he may get more than he bargained for.

Fresco from Herculaneum. Courtesy of Stefano Bolognini.

CHECKING THE ROMAN *WANT ADS*

While many churches today give Christian goody bags for visitors containing packets of hot cocoa, logo-laden coffee mugs, and flashlights studded with adages such as "May the light of Christ shine on you," early Christians preferred the subtle tactic of cross examination. As the third-century document the *Apostolic Tradition* put it:

> New converts to the faith, who are to be admitted as hearers of the word, shall first be brought to the teachers before the people assemble. And they shall be examined as to their reason for embracing the faith...Inquiry shall then be made as to the nature of their life; whether a man has a wife or is a slave, etc.[12]

If this man chooses to be a Christian after undergoing cross-examination without receiving chocolaty treats, he may have to change careers—though, due to his high status, he may be entitled to continue bathing and

"Most people convert to a new religion because their friends and relatives already have done so—when their social ties to the religious group outweigh their ties to outsiders."[33]

eating all day so long as he served as the patron of the local church and pulled strings for his new Christian clients when necessary.

According to the *Apostolic Tradition*, "Inquiry shall likewise be made about the professions and trades of those who are brought to be admitted to the faith." To save ourselves from suspense, people would need to check the Roman Want Ads if they wanted to become a Christian while simultaneously being: a "sculptor or painter," "actor or pantomimist," "charioteer," "gladiator or trainer of gladiators," "military commander or civic magistrate," "[somebody] who does things not to be named [perhaps the modern equivalent of someone who wears socks with sandals]," "magician," "enchanter," "astrologer," "diviner," "soothsayer," or, in case that was not clear enough, "a user of magic." Each of these professions or careers was prohibited by Christian churches. Last but not least, the profession of teaching—of young children at any rate—was highly discouraged: "A teacher of young children had best desist, but if he has no other occupation, he may be permitted to continue."[13] Because teaching in the ancient world was so intertwined with pagan history, beliefs, and rituals, it was best to avoid it altogether.

Writing in the third century, Bishop Cyprian of Carthage argued that it was better for those who teach the art of acting to be jobless and supported by the church community than to "be defiled by such base and infamous contamination" as acting, in part because male actors had to play the part of a woman. If the church was financially unable to support the teacher, Cyprian said his church would gladly pick up the bill.[34]

A DAY IN THE LIFE OF A BATH-STOKER

With such a long list of unacceptable careers, one wonders what kinds of prospects were available for converts. Here the evidence is ambiguous, but it's best not to get one's hopes up. About ninety percent of Christians were illiterate.[14] That's right—perhaps less than ten percent of Christians could read or write in the early centuries of the church. But even if they could read, early Christians could hardly have afforded the books and scribes necessary to maintain a library—and if they suffered from near- or far-sightedness, the books would have been worthless since glasses would not be invented for more than a thousand years. Prohibitions as found in the *Apostolic Tradition* only made matters more difficult for Christians who aspired to become Roman white-collar workers by denying teaching opportunities to adults and learning opportunities to children.

Although the feisty Christian author Tertullian boasted at the end of the second century that Christians had risen to every sector of society save the Roman priesthood,[15] his contemporary Origen conceded that many Christians were "wool-workers…cobblers…laundry-workers and the most illiterate yokels [imaginable]."[16]In all likelihood, many Christians during the first couple of centuries "were handworkers."[17]Which is to say that many Christians were uneducated and illiterate "craftspeople, artisans, and small traders."[18] For such workers, other than festival days, they toiled seven days of week, as there were no Sundays off from work until Constantine became emperor in the early fourth century. For these Christians, work began at dawn and ended at dusk. It was not generally safe to be outside alone at dark (and there were no lamp posts to light the streets), so many people would return to their tiny and mice-infested flats for the night unless business required otherwise. Their meals would have been low in calories and fat, but not because they were watching their figures—such was all they could afford.

> Writing in the second half of the second century, Christian apologist Athenagoras of Athens conceded that the church was disproportionally full of "uneducated persons…artisans, and old women."[35]

Like Jesus the carpenter, Peter the fisherman, Simon the tanner, and Paul the tentmaker, we can envision ancient Christians such as Sabina the stoneworker, Holconius the cabinet-maker, Iris the barmaid, and Primus the bath-stoker.[19] Ancient Christians were chamber servants, dealers in huts, picklers, butchers, merchants, and pig sellers. Contrary to what we so often envision of the earliest Christians, their lives were not at all glamorous. We can't really describe such laborers as "the working middle class" because that term implies more wealth, education, mobility, and security than they actually had—or ever daydreamed was possible. The lives of these early Christians were very modest, but they were not at the bottom rung of society. That category was reserved exclusively for the slave.

A SOCIETY OF SLAVES

Slavery was part and parcel of the ancient world, but it was not racially based as it was in the United States. As representatives of the Roman population in general, a good percentage of early Christians were slaves, former slaves (called *freedmen*), or masters. In fact, "There were more slaves in the Roman empire than in any previous society."[20] Although we casually skim over such stories in the New Testament due to our sanitized understanding of the ancient world, Jesus and the earliest

Christians would have interacted with slaves and slave owners on a daily basis. It's hard to read a page of the New Testament, in fact, without coming across an explicit reference or literary allusion to slaves, slavery, and slave owning. On average in the Roman Empire, every fifth or sixth person was a slave, meaning that there wasn't a hamlet, village, or town in the ancient world that didn't have slaves. In Rome, however, the capital of the empire and perhaps the largest city in the world, a third of the entire population were slaves. On a given day in ancient Rome, you would have come across dozens, if not hundreds, of them.

Although some slaves lived better than free people and ascended to the heights of Roman society, let's not kid ourselves: Slavery was a living hell for countless men, women, and children—Christians included, of course. Even though those living in the city generally fared better than rural slaves, who often were forced to work in chains and were given meager rations, slaves in the city were still regarded as property and could live or die at the whims of their owners. One of the most common forms of slavery in urban environments was domestic or household slavery. Domestic slaves lived in the home of their masters in close quarters with other slaves. As legally owned property, they cooked, cleaned, served, guarded the house, ran errands, fetched water, served as wet nurses, scraped the skin of their owner's backs at the baths, washed their feet, watched after their children, and sometimes balanced the books. They also accompanied the master and his family when traveling in public in order to maintain the master's honor, which was the currency of ancient society and only available to the wealthy and powerful. (Virtually by definition, slaves had no honor.)

> "The lowest legal status of all was the slave's. Greek philosophers considered him something less than human. Roman law regarded him as a piece of property, and the thousands of slaves who worked as chattel gangs on ships, farms, road construction, or mining were treated as nothing but a commodity."[36]

THE UNDERBELLY OF THE ANCIENT WORLD

Alongside slavery came unchecked sexual abuse. It was a normal feature of life in the Roman world for masters of the house, the *patres familias*, to demand sex from their female slaves as well as to defile enslaved boys. Although illegal and morally revolting today, Roman law sanctioned such intercourse and society did not consider it immoral. Sex between a master and his wife, after all, was designed mostly for procreation, and marriages were oftentimes unhappy political alliances that had nothing to do with emotion or love. They were primarily about preserving (and increasing) property—the principle source of wealth in the ancient world.

With his wife effectively partitioned from him, the master could easily turn to his legally owned and defenseless property for sexual gratification. The fact that master and mistress did not typically share a bedroom only made this course of action easy and inevitable.

The Romans had a rather bleak take on male sexuality. For them, the male libido was a raging river that had to be properly channeled so that it didn't inundate the countryside. For the Romans, this meant redirecting the libido away from a woman of honor and toward a woman (or man, as same-sex penetration was widespread) of no honor—usually a slave. It was a common belief that female slaves and prostitutes "drain[ed] off excess male sexual energy as a sewer drained off waste."[21] Accounting for more than half of the slave population, argues classicist Kyle Harper, females "were devastatingly vulnerable" and "bore the brunt of sexual abuse."[22] The prominent Christian author Jerome, the translator of the most famous biblical version in the world, acknowledged this Roman belief at the turn of the fifth century when he wrote that "men's chastity goes unchecked…free permission is given to lust to range the brothels and to have slave girls."[23]

> "It is with justice, we believe, that the condition of slavery is the result of sin. And this is why we do not find the word 'slave' in any part of Scripture until righteous Noah branded the sin of his son with this name. It is a name, therefore, introduced by sin and not by nature."[37]

In the underbelly of the ancient world, Christian slaves were not exempt from their master's repressed sexual energy. The fact that most Roman emperors, including Tiberius—who was ruler during Jesus's entire ministry—took out their unrestrained lust on helpless male and female slaves was no secret.[24] Early Christian leaders would not have been unaware that many female (and boy) slaves were the sexual targets of their masters. In fact, certain scholars believe that 1 Peter's exhortation for slaves to "accept the authority of your masters with all deference, not only those who are kind and gentle but also those who are harsh" (2:18) implies a tacit acceptance of sexual slavery. Whether or not that is true, the culture of sexual slavery was prevalent: Apostles like Paul would have seen it up close while a guest at a wealthy Roman estate or while pastoring slaves and slave owners. As historian of slavery Jennifer Glancy explains, "Paul would inevitably have encountered slaves whose obligations included sexual relations with their owners and those to whom their owners permitted sexual access."[25]

Paul himself made frequent mention of both sex and slavery in his letters, though strangely, Glancy notes, he never explicitly condemned sex with one's slave "to be inconsistent with the Christian ethos,"[26] unless one interprets his rejection of "fornication" to include such an act. Perhaps Paul addressed this issue so decisively in person that he did not need to write about it in personal letters, perhaps he felt it unwise to teach contrary to the laws and customs of Rome, or perhaps he thought Abraham's sexual propriety over his slave girl Hagar, among many other examples in the Old Testament, gave *de facto* approval to the practice. However we interpret this argument from silence—and we have to be as cautious as we are candid—legislation was not enacted against this practice for centuries. The eminent historian Peter Brown provides a rather dreary commentary on this issue:

> The leaders of the Christian church...followed the philosophers in condemning the anomaly of the Roman 'double standard,' which had punished the wife for adultery while accepting unfaithfulness in a husband. But the clergy showed themselves as little prepared as the philosophers had been to overturn the institution of household slavery. By their hesitation on that issue, they doomed themselves from the outset to an honorable ineffectiveness on the issue of marital fidelity. Most infidelity took the form of sleeping with one's own slaves: it was simply one assertion, among so many, of the master's power over the bodies of his dependents.[27]

It was not until around the fourth century that legislation was enacted against Christian masters having sex with their slaves.[28] But even then, perhaps a remnant of the church's "honorable ineffectiveness," the habit was too hard for many Christian Romans to break. We see an example of this in a Christian master's reply to Bishop Augustine of Hippo after being pressed about sleeping with his slave: "Would you rather," the man retorted incredulously, "[that] I sleep with someone else's wife?"—as if his only options were to have sex with his wife or take the honor of another married woman, but not to divert his sexual energy away from his legally owned property. "Can I not," he continued in disbelief, "do what I want in my own house?"[29] For this Christian at any rate, he was raising a question that had been safeguarded by Roman law and custom for centuries.

NOT YOUR MOTHER'S SUNDAY SCHOOL CLASS

The study of the daily life of early Christianity bruises our modern conscience. Widespread malnutrition, incredibly high percentages of illiteracy, unquestioned patriarchy, sexual slavery—this was not what we were taught in Sunday school! Despite what we envision from bucolic pictures on church walls, the world of early Christianity was nothing like the modernized, secure, and convenience-laden world of today. There were no police officers to protect one's property, no weekends to recharge one's batteries, and virtually no way to read, let alone possess, the Bible for oneself. For many early Christians, life was unfair, labor was backbreaking, and liberty was make-believe. While we panic in the modern world over where to take our vacations, many early Christians would have stressed over where they would find their next meal, or whether they should risk life or limb by refusing the sexual advances of their legal owner. Despite the discomfort we feel as we ponder these grim realities, let us not grow weary in coming face-to-face with our history. Instead, let it shape us in the present and mold us into people who do not naively look back to our sanitized past, but ponder how God advances his kingdom by means of the messy people and messy institution that is the church.

ENDNOTES

1 According to historian Carolyn Osiek, "Defecation and urination were not considered private functions." See her "Family Matters," in *Christian Origins*, vol. 1, A People's History of Christianity, ed. Richard Horsley (Minneapolis: Fortress, 2013), 205.

2 In both of these biblical quotations, there is also an element of shame and dishonor.

3 See "Parasites Increased during Roman Times," *Past Horizons*, January 9, 2016, http://www.pasthorizonspr.com/index.php/archives/01/2016/parasites-increased-during-roman-times and Piers Mitchell, "Human Parasites in the Roman Empire: Health Consequences of Conquering an Empire," *Parasitology*, FirstView no. 1 (2016): 1–11.

4 Quoted in David Horrell, *Becoming Christian: Essays on 1 Peter and the Making of Christian Identity* (London and New York: Bloomsbury T&T Clark, 2013), 107.

5 Steven Friesen, "Injustice or God's Will? Early Christian Explanations of Poverty," in *Wealth and Poverty in Early Church and Society*, ed. Susan Holman (Grand Rapids, MI: Baker Academic, 2008), 30.

6 David Fiensy, "What Would You Do for a Living?" in *Handbook of Early Christianity: Social Science Approaches*, ed. Anthony Blasi, Jean Duhaime, and Paul-Andre Turcotte (Walnut Creek, CA: Altamira Press, 2002), 564.

7 Mary Beard, *SPQR: A History of Ancient Rome* (New York: Liveright Publishing, 2015), 46.

8 Osiek, "Family Matters," in *Christian Origins*, 203.

9 Beard, *SPQR*, 313.

10 Matthew Hartnett, *By Roman Hands: Inscriptions and Graffiti for Students of Latin* (Newburyport, MA: The Focus Classical Library, 2008), 61.

11 Kyle Harper, *From Shame to Sin: The Christian Transformation of Sexual Morality in Late Antiquity* (Cambridge, MA: Harvard University Press, 2013), 3.

12 Hippolytus, "The Apostolic Tradition," in *The Apostolic Tradition of Hippolytus*, ed. B. S. Easton (Cambridge: Cambridge University Press, 1934), 42.

13 Hippolytus, "Apostolic Tradition 15.1–3," in *The Apostolic Tradition*, 42.

14 Harry Gamble, *Books and Readers in the Early Church: A History of Early Christian Texts* (New Haven: Yale University Press, 1995), 10.

15 See Tertullian, *Apology* 37.

16 Origen, "Contra Celsum 3.58," in *Origen: Contra Celsum*, trans. Henry Chadwick (Cambridge: Cambridge University Press, 1980), 167.

17 Fiensy, "What Would You Do For a Living?" in *Handbook*, 565.

18 Gamble, *Books and Readers*, 5.

19 See Peter Oakes, *Reading Romans in Pompeii* (Minneapolis, MN: Fortress Press, 2009), 1–45.

20 Ibid., 113

21 Carter Lindberg, "Luther's Struggle with Social-Ethical Issues," in *The Cambridge Companion to Martin Luther*, ed. Donald McKim (Cambridge: Cambridge University Press, 2003), 169. Lindberg is speaking specifically of medieval sexual mores, which were a direct product of ancient ones.

22 Harper, *From Shame to Sin*, 45.

23 Jerome, *Epistle* 77.3, quoted in Jennifer Glancy, *Slavery in Early Christianity* (Minneapolis, MN: Fortress, 2006), 58.

24 See Suetonius's description of Tiberius's lust in *Homosexuality in Greece and Rome: A Sourcebook of Basic Documents*, ed. Thomas Hubbard (Berkeley, CA: University of California Press, 2003), 387–388.

25 Glancy, *Slavery in Early Christianity*, 52.

26 Glancy, *Slavery in Early Christianity*, 70. De Wet also notes that "the New Testament is surprisingly silent on the issue of the sexual abuse of slaves," in *Preaching Bondage*, 224. See also Harper, *Slavery in the Late Roman World*, 322.

27 Peter Brown, *The Body and Society: Men, Women, and Sexual Renunciation in Early Christianity* (New York: Columbia University Press, 1988), 23.

28 John Chrysostom preached, "I, myself, am saying that it is adultery all the same when [a master] has sex with any woman—whether she is openly a prostitute, a slave girl, or any other woman without a husband—it is wicked and concupiscent," in De Wet, *Preaching Bondage*, 231. See also Harper, *From Shame to Sin*, 8.

29 Quoted in Harper, *Slavery in the Late Roman World*, 296.

30 Peter Brown, *Through the Eye of a Needle* (Princeton, NJ: Princeton University Press, 2012), 8

31 Helen Rhee, *Loving the Poor, Saving the Rich*, 22.

32 Jerome Carcopino, *Daily Life in Ancient Rome* (New Haven, CT: Yale University Press, 2003; 2nd ed.), 23.

33 Rodney Stark, *The Rise of Christianity* [New York: HarperSanFrancisco, 1997], 133

34 Saint Cyprian, *Letters (1-81)*, Letter 2, The Fathers of the Church, vol. 51 (Washington, D.C.: The Catholic University Press of America, 2013), 5.

35 See Athenagoras, "Plea for the Christians 11," in ANCF, vol. 2, *Justin Martyr and Athenagoras*, 387

36 John Stambaugh and David Balch, *The Social World of the First Christians* (London: SPCK, 1986), 124.

37 Augustine, "The City of God," NPNF, 2:411

Chapter 2

LEADING WITH A LIMP—FLAWED LEADERSHIP

He was not the easiest man to get along with. Overbearing, contentious, and rather sensitive, the apostle Paul had more flesh on his blessed bones than many Christians care to admit. As excerpts from his New Testament letters confirm, this was a man not above resorting to threats, not above lashing out in frustration, and not above shaming his disciples into submission. Though sanctified by the blood of the Lamb, Paul the Saint was simultaneously Paul the Sinner. Routinely rejected by the people he led, Paul struggled to strike a balance between fatherly criticism and motherly compassion. Most trying, he was a man of principle—to a fault. If Paul's letters had not been rightly recognized as divinely inspired Scripture, we might question his rabblerousing rhetoric and heavy-handed behavior. What are we to do, for instance, with his eyebrow-raising exhortation: "I wish those who unsettle you would castrate themselves!" (Gal. 5:12)? What are we to do with his strong condemnation of the Jewish people in light of Christian anti-Semitism: "the Jews...displease God...they have constantly been filling up the measure of their sins; but God's wrath has overtaken them at last" (1 Thess. 2:15–16)? And what are we to do with Paul's direct command for slaves to remain in bondage to their masters despite the freedom he said they had in Christ: "Slaves, obey your earthly masters with fear and trembling" (Eph. 6:5)?

Paul's reputation had preceded his entrance into the church. While he agonized in a dark room in Damascus after losing his sight on the way to persecuting followers of "the Way," a Christian named Ananias was trying to talk Jesus out of allowing this tormentor from being baptized. "Lord," Ananias responded in a state of sheer disbelief, "I have heard from many about this man" (Acts 9:13)—to which his bodily language must have added, "and what I have heard ain't been pretty." After baptizing Paul and infusing him with the Holy Spirit, Ananias released this man of strife onto the world. Those who heard Paul praise Jesus Christ as God's Son immediately thereafter, the book of Acts reports, "were amazed, and said, 'Is not this the man who made [such] havoc in Jerusalem?" (9:21). Rather than celebrate Paul's change of heart with the kiss of peace or at least a halfhearted handshake, fellow Christians "were all afraid of him...[and] did not believe that he was a disciple" (9:26).

THE BEAT GOES ON

Like the apostle Paul, one of the most famous sinful saints of the church, Christian leaders have always led with a limp. Truth is, there has never been a generation of Christian leaders that has not fallen into great shame, warranted public condemnation, or created church division. Besides worshiping, serving, and tithing, sinning is what we Christians do best—and our leaders do it about as well as anyone. Though I hasten to add that our leaders aren't completely bad, they certainly aren't completely good—and it's been this way since the beginning. Because we almost always emphasize the sure and sin-free strides of our earliest leaders, let's look as their limps in this chapter.

CELEBRITY SHOWDOWN

Though rarely discussed today, the apparent dislike of the early church's most prominent leaders was legendary among ancient Christians. In what may be the oldest letter in the New Testament, the apostle Paul openly lambasted Peter for his hypocritical religious practices, illustrating that not all that glitters in the Christian world is gold. Paul, possibly bypassing the principle in Matthew 18 exhorting us to air our grievances privately before publicly, seemingly had an axe to grind with the leading apostle of the church. In the Letter to the Galatians, Paul openly asserted, "When Peter came to Antioch, I opposed him to his face, because he was clearly in the wrong" (2:11). What was Peter doing that was so "clearly in the wrong"? For fear of Jewish Christian reprisal, Peter had stopped eating with Gentile Christians—effectively paying lip service to the paramount teaching of Jesus that Christianity was for Gentiles as much as it was for Jews. But Paul, not one to turn a blind eye to matters of the gospel or to back down from a church fight, boldly wrote, "I said to Peter in front of them all, 'You are a Jew, yet you live like a Gentile and not like a Jew. How is it, then, that you force Gentiles to follow Jewish customs?" (2:14).

***The Apostle Paul* by Rembrandt.**

This was a loaded question. The New Testament doesn't record Peter's response to it. Perhaps it was red-hot anger. Perhaps Peter turned the tables on Paul and began pointing fingers at *his* questionable actions—such as circumcising Timothy even after he had taught that "there is no benefit in being circumcised" (Gal. 5:2). Or perhaps Peter, recalling the teachings of Jesus, turned his cheek. However Peter reacted, we do know how early Christians interpreted this encounter. Although some of them owned up to the awkwardness of the story, and one Jewish Christian used it as a way to illustrate that Peter and Paul were "enemies,"[1] others turned to damage control. Word was not to get out that the leaders of the Christian faith were fighting. Long before there were public relations agents for celebrities, it appears, there were Christian theologians trying to whitewash the indiscretions of their idols. A second-century theologian named Clement of Alexandria, for instance, argued that the Peter (literally "Cephas") referred to in this incident was not the apostle Peter. Who was this named yet unknown Peter being referred to, then? Who knows, but he could not have been Peter, the "rock" on whom Christ decided to build his church, because he was perfect—or so the thinking goes.

According to 2 Peter 3:16, the apostle Paul's "letters contain some things that are hard to understand."

***St. Peter in Prison* by Rembrandt.**

While Christians went to great lengths to explain away the obvious, non-Christians took this passage at face value. They made the deceptively straightforward argument that Peter and Paul just didn't like each other. That simple. Only it wasn't: For such critics, the fact that Peter and Paul fought with one another was sure-fire proof that Christianity was false. Porphyry, a third-century pagan philosopher from what is now Lebanon, was deeply critical of this scandal between the two greatest leaders of the church. He wrote in disgust in his book *Against the Christians*: "Paul and Peter waged a childish contest...Paul envied the virtues of Peter, and wrote...against him, pugnaciously."[2] In fact, from what we can piece together from his writings (none of his works survive intact because they were destroyed when Christians came into power), Porphyry was less critical of Christ and more so of Christ's followers. As he wrote in a book titled *Philosophy from Oracles*, "the gods have pronounced Christ to have been extremely devout...whereas the Christians...are polluted and contaminated."[3]Things have not changed much, for this is a common argument today and the stuff of hypocritical religion—the founder was good, but his followers leave much to be desired.

Rather than own up to the awkward, if not embarrassing, feud between the apostles Peter and Paul, the most learned commentators of early Christianity attempted to undermine Porphyry by clutching at intellectual straws. Chrysostom and Jerome, two otherwise critically minded thinkers not afraid to air their grievances, argued that Peter and Paul *staged* this fight. It was all a practical joke. As Jerome reasoned, "how...could Paul venture to rebuke publicly the greatest of the apostles so resolutely and firmly, unless Peter consented [beforehand]?"[4] Rather than getting into a public debate, Jerome rationalized, Peter and Paul faked a "holy dispute."[5] Like two boxers seeking to polarize their fans before a match but who afterwards go out for an intimate and friendly dinner, Peter and Paul played the public for the sake of proclaiming the gospel. Though dismissing as an old wives' tale, Clement of Alexandria's argument that the Peter mentioned in this story was not really Peter Jerome still couldn't bring himself to accept that the two greatest leaders of early Christianity quarreled in public. Rather than admit that one, if not both, of these men simply made a mistake and sinned, one of the greatest minds of Christianity opted for suspension of reason.

We should pause here to reflect on the well-intended but poorly miscalculated actions of our most celebrated Christian leaders after the era of the apostles. Unfortunately, as we have discussed at length, Christians have not often advanced beyond Chrysostom's and Jerome's thinking on this matter; we're still in the habit of sticking our heads in the sand when it comes to acknowledging the failures of our leaders. We see to what great lengths the church fathers went to cover up the indiscretions of the apostles only to recognize that their inclination to do so only made matters worse—first by continuing the nostalgic narrative that the earliest Christians were flawless and, second, by not recognizing that our desire to conceal such flaws pushes non-Christians farther away from the faith.

THE CHURCH GETS SERIOUS

Because all believers are sinful saints, the brawl between Peter and Paul was just the beginning of the squabbles, scandals, and showdowns that would characterize early Christian leadership. As Christianity developed, a very definable church leadership structure emerged. What Saint Paul implanted in seed form in the Pastoral Epistles of 1 Timothy and Titus ripened into the ordained offices of deacon, priest, and bishop (though the exact relationship among these terms is highly debated even to this day). Under this clerical configuration, the bishops were the true powerbrokers of early Christianity. They oversaw all of the priests and deacons in

Besides the major offices of bishop, priest (also called presbyter), and deacon, there were many minor ones: sub-deacons, acolytes, exorcists, readers, doorkeepers, and widows. In the early church, women were also ordained as deaconesses, a practice that eventually fell into disuse.

their dioceses, and their word on any particular matter was the law of the land, for they were the human representatives of Christ himself. This representation worked well for some dioceses, but there were plenty of bishops whose ego or libido got in the way of God's good design for church leadership.

BRASS-KNUCKLES THEOLOGY

The church was nothing if it wasn't a seedbed of controversy, and many of the controversies that took place in the early centuries occurred at the upper echelons of leadership. Though there were plenty of exceptions, many bishops, like two alpha males marking their territory, preferred a chest fight over a prayerful dialogue. It was one thing for a bishop to oversee the customs in his own diocese, but it was sometimes another when those customs were challenged by another bishop. In the year 155, Bishop Polycarp of Smyrna (in modern Turkey) was visiting Bishop Anicetus of Rome. All was well with their souls—until the conversation turned to religion. For quite some time, there had been a growing rift between the way Eastern and Western Christians celebrated the most sacred day of the Christian calendar: Easter. (That's right, Christians have never fully agreed on when to celebrate the most important day of the year.) The Eastern Christians, tracing their practice to the tradition they received from the apostle John—rumored to have lived the remainder of his life in Ephesus—celebrated Easter on the fourteenth day of the Jewish month of Nisan.

Saint Polycarp. Courtesy of Wellcome Library, London.

Coming from the Latin word for "fourteen," these *Quartodecimans* celebrated Easter at the same time Jews celebrated Passover. Western

Christians, by contrast, shuddered at the very suggestion that Jesus's resurrection was celebrated on a Jewish holiday. Didn't the book of Hebrews say that the "law has but a shadow of the good things to come instead of the true form of these realities" (10:1)? Based on biblical passages such as these, many early Christians like Justin Martyr believed that Judaism was "already obsolete."[6] Tracing their practice to the so-named Synoptic Gospels and the traditions handed down to them, Christian bishops in the West observed Easter on the Sunday after the first full moon after the vernal equinox, regardless of when the Jewish festival of Passover occurred—a practice still followed by Western churches, which was canonized at the Council of Nicea in 325.

The discussion between Polycarp and Anicetus was at a standstill. As ancient Christian bishop Eusebius later stated in his church history book, "Anicetus could not persuade Polycarp…nor did Polycarp persuade Anicetus."[7] Although these two bishops begrudgingly consented to an "'agree to disagree' policy,"[8] this dispute festered like an untreated blister until it finally oozed over a few decades later. By this time there were three major bishops involved: Irenaeus of Lyons (in France), Polycrates of Ephesus (in Turkey), and Victor of Rome. Polycrates struck first. In a letter addressed to Pope Victor, Polycrates boldly refused to make any compromises with Western Christians:

> The Synoptic Gospels are Matthew, Mark, and Luke. They are so called because they follow a similar chronology and timeline. John's Gospel, by contrast, makes use of different sources. Whereas Jesus eats a Passover meal in the Synoptic Gospels, for instance, the Last Supper is eaten before the Passover in John's Gospel.

> I,…after spending sixty-five years in the Lord's service and conversing with Christians from all parts of the world, and going carefully through all Holy Scripture, am not scared of [your] threats. Better people than I have said: 'We must obey God rather than men.'[9]

Polycrates was delightfully temperamental. He didn't care what title was imprinted on Victor's business card. Pope or not, the successor to the blessed apostle Peter or not, Polycrates was only going to follow the straight and narrow path of holy tradition. If it was good enough for the apostle John to celebrate Easter on Nisan 14, it was darn well good enough for him.

Still, Pope Victor was no pushover. He had ascended to the most prestigious post in Christianity, and he was not going to back down to the likes of any other bishop. In his response to Polycrates, Victor went straight for the jugular. As Eusebius later reported, "Victor…attempted at one stroke to cut off from the common unity of all the Asian dioceses."

Rather than negotiate with fellow church leaders, Victor turned to brass-knuckles theology. As Eusebius explained, Victor "pilloried [Asian bishops] in letters in which he announced the total excommunication of all his fellow-Christians there."[10] That's right—"total excommunication." Victor was willing to condemn more than half of the body of Christ for failing to celebrate the resurrection the same day he and his Western tradition celebrated it. Had it not been for the sensible pleas of Bishop Irenaeus, who managed to calm down the volatile Victor, the Eastern and Western churches would have divided much earlier than they did—which eventually did happen in the Middle Ages.

Fortunately for us, Victor did not get his way. In fact, there are many other fine examples of bishops in the early church, like Irenaeus, who sought peace and reconciliation amidst troubling times. As easy as it is for us to point fingers and assign blame to earlier believers, they were very much caught between a rock and a hard place. Although the multicultural, multidenominational, and multifaceted world we inhabit allows us to see the value of differing cultures, differing denominations, and differing opinions, such was not the case in ancient times. Leaders had to make split-second decisions without the advantages of leadership classes, without friendships with clergy of other denominations, and without a culture of tolerance and acceptance. Believing themselves to be gatekeepers of life and death entrusted to preserve the singular deposit of truth, they dared not endanger the spiritual welfare of their flocks just because their beliefs offended certain people or were regarded as unpopular.

'A LIVELY CONTROVERSY'

In addition to the feud among bishops in the second century, other sordid stories abounded when it came to early church leadership. One such dispute—what Eusebius adorably called "a lively controversy"[11]—involved the bishops of Rome and Cyprian in the third century. Their names were Stephen and Cyprian, respectively, and they were bishops of two of the most influential dioceses in the West. Like rams in a fight for death, these two powerful and stubborn bishops locked horns over the issue of how to rehabilitate lapsed or schismatic Christians. The very fact that these two men were butting heads over this issue indicates that there was a prior dispute. The

> In his interpretation of Matthew 22:1–14, Novatian explained to Cyprian: "God is passionate, but He also demands—indeed, He strictly demands—the observance of His precepts. He invites guests to His wedding banquet, but the man who wears no wedding garment He has cast out by his hands and feet from the assembly of the saints. He has prepared heaven, but He has also prepared [hell]."[30]

issue at hand revolved around the so-called Novatianist Schism, named after an interim bishop in Rome named Novatian. After the martyrdom of Bishop Fabian of Rome in January of 250, Novatian became acting bishop of the Roman diocese in order to provide guidance to the persecuted church. It was a dangerous time, and Christian leaders were doing their darndest to keep the faith intact. Not surprising given that his predecessor, and the very man who had ordained him to the priesthood, had been hunted down like a rabbit and killed, Novatian took this issue personally. Rather than allowing backsliders into the church, Novatian "dug in his heels"[12] and turned his back on them. Novatian, after all, was a hard-nosed rigorist, believing that the acceptance of apostates back into the church even on their deathbeds was an affront to Christ. In his second letter to Bishop Cyprian, he queried, "What will happen to the fear of God if pardon is so readily granted to sinners?"[13]

Novatian's tactics were largely unpopular, though they did endear him to some conservative clerics. When persecution ceased at the death of Emperor Diocletian in 251, Roman Christians washed their hands of Novatian and appointed a more easygoing bishop named Cornelius to the throne of Peter. Novatian, however, had learned some tricks on the interim trade, and he agreed to be consecrated by three separate bishops as the true bishop of Rome. Not surprising given the political climate of the Roman Empire, a council of bishops excommunicated Novatian and his followers in the spring of 251.

As time went on and some of Novatian's purebred sheep wanted to return to the goats in the Catholic Church, leaders had to determine the best way to rehabilitate these schismatic Christians back into the fold of Christ. The most pressing issue had to do with baptism. Did a Novatianist Christian have to be re-baptized into the Catholic Church since the priest or bishop who baptized that person was a bastard Christian cleric? Stephen, the current bishop of Rome, took a moderate approach to this issue. As long as a Novatianist was baptized in the name of the Father, Son, and Holy Spirit, he explained, it didn't matter who performed the ceremony. It's even rumored that the old devil was willing to readmit heretics from the false church of Marcion—whom many early Christians regarded as Satan incarnate. All that Bishop Stephen requested from heretical

In its two-thousand year history, the Roman papacy has witnessed a number of so-called *antipopes*. These are rival popes consecrated as bishops of Rome in opposition to existing bishops. At its worst, there was a time when there were actually three popes at the same time. According to historical records, Novatian was likely the third antipope. During his time as antipope from 251–258, he outlived four different bishops of Rome until dying as a martyr.

Christians returning to the Catholic Church was the mere laying on of hands. That was good enough for Stephen, and he was ready to excommunicate any bishops who disagreed with him—leading us to conclude that this bishop of Rome hadn't learned much since the time of the volatile Victor.

Bishop Cyprian, however, was a stickler for these sorts of things. What else should we expect from a man who tenaciously taught that "you can't have God as a father unless you have the Church as a mother"?[14] Challenging the authority of Bishop Stephen of Rome to take such a lax position, Cyprian appealed to preceding councils of bishops, which had ruled that heretics seeking to return to the Catholic Church must be baptized again. He wrote that those who had been "dipped among the heretics"—notice that he intentionally refrained from using the word "baptized" since he thought legitimate baptism only occurred within the Catholic Church—were defiled by contaminated water. Continuing on, Cyprian argued that those "who come to us out of heresy are not re-baptized by us; they are baptized."[15] When African bishops took a letter confirming this practice to Bishop Stephen, the latter rebuffed them. He didn't even grant them an audience—or, for all we can gather, he didn't even give the bishops a cup of cold water. Instead, Stephen sent a white-hot letter by post, calling Cyprian "a false Christ" and "a false apostle."[16] While boiling over in anger, historian Geoffrey Willis explains, Stephen also wrote to the bishops in Asia Minor, "threatening to excommunicate the whole Church there if it persisted in its support of the practice of rebaptism."[17]

Bishop Dionysius, watching the unity of the church fissure before his very eyes, tried to talk some sense into the hotheaded pope. It's reassuring to know that when one leader flies off the handle, there is always another one nearby to calm things down. This time it was Dionysius; at other times it was others. If it weren't for the fact that both Stephen and Cyprian were soon to die, these two men could have divided the entire church over this issue. For one thing is certain: The occupant of the Chair of Peter was nothing if he wasn't tenaciously holding to his position. He, whoever that might be from year to year, was not going to change his mind. A century after this fight between the bishop of Rome and bishop of Carthage, for instance, the bishop of Rome was still mouthing threats against any bishop who insisted on Novatianists being re-baptized by Catholic clergy. Writing to a Spanish bishop in the late fourth century regarding this issue, Bishop Siricius of Rome warned: It is not allowed "for you to deviate from that path, if you do not wish to be separated from our company by synodal sentence,"[18] by which he meant formal excommunication and separation from God.

As was becoming painfully clear during the reign of Stephen, it was the bishop of Rome who was gradually gaining the head seat at a previously roundtable of bishops. And once he did so, there was no going back. The occupant of the Chair of Peter was becoming *primer inter pares*, "the first among equals." In a world that was only getting more hectic and heretical by the moment, it was increasingly more expedient for one cock to rule the roost. As any good Christian might select, the weapon of choice when it came to asserting the bishop of Rome's God-given authority was the Bible itself. Like a man brandishing a loaded gun, Stephen was the first bishop of Rome to use Matthew 16:18 to silence his opposition. Although Cyprian disagreed with Stephen's strategy, he knew he had been outplayed, for Stephen was the successor to the Throne of Peter in a way that neither he nor any other bishop could be. For to whom else did Jesus say, "you are Peter, and on this rock I will build my church…I will give *you* [singular in Greek] the keys the keys of the kingdom of heaven, and whatever *you* [again, singular] bind on earth shall be bound in heaven" (Matt. 16:18–19)?

The answer to this question was becoming clear enough in the West: to no one but Peter and his successors. Adapting Roman legal language of adoption and heredity, the bishops of Rome had resolutely reasoned that they were the sole legal heirs of the apostle Peter. Although it's easy for us to think these popes were on one big power trip, it's possible they were just seeking to faithfully understand the Bible in light of their contemporary cultural contexts. As historian of antiquity Christian Hornung explains: "The law of succession alone permits [Peter] *and his successors* to apply the biblical passage of Matthew 16:18–19 to Roman bishops. Thus, as the deceased and his heir become one, Peter and the Roman bishop become one."[19] According to Roman law, in other words, the heir inherited all of the rights, authorities, and privileges of the deceased, meaning that the occupant of Peter's chair, who in turn was keeping Jesus's chair warm while he remained at the right hand of the Father, exercised full responsibilities. He was, in short, the *vicar* of Christ, the earthly representative of the heavenly Jesus.

'THE EAR-TICKLER OF LADIES'

Given the burden of biblical support, cultural context, and common approval, it's not surprising that the bishop of Rome was acquiring unrivaled authority among Christians. Although it might seem reasonable to infer that church scandals would cease once everyone—at least in the West—agreed where the buck would stop, church scandals at the upper level of leadership did not disappear. If anything, they only increased. One such story of scandal revolved around the most influential Roman bishop in early Christianity. His birth name was Damasus, but his nickname was more revealing: *matronarum auriscalpius*, "the ear-tickler of ladies." Coming into power with a bang in the late fourth

> According to many scholars, the understanding of the bishop of Rome as *pope*—and thus leader of the church at large—solidified in the late fourth century. Although it's technically anachronistic to refer to the bishop of Rome as the pope before then, it's a common practice.

century while in his early sixties, this pope carried a big stick and a grand vision for the most sacred office on earth. His papacy, however, swarmed with scandal from the beginning.

As providence would have it, Damasus was not the only candidate for the papacy in 366, and his rival, a man named Ursinus, was proving to be an intractable opponent. Something short of holy warfare broke out between the faction of Damasus and that of Ursinus. According to one report, Damasus "hired a gang of thugs to storm the Julian basilica [where Ursinus and his cronies were meeting], routing the Ursinians in a three-day massacre."[20] So vicious and violent had the papal war become, notes one early historian, that "State intervention was required in the interests of public order."[21] The brutal battle for the holiest office on earth had gotten so bad, in fact, that even pagans were noticing. Writing in 366, the pagan Ammianus Marcellinus candidly observed:

> Considering the ostentatious luxury of life in the city it is only natural that those who are ambitious of enjoying it should engage in the most strenuous competition to attain their goal. Once they have reached it [the bishopric of Rome] they are assured of rich gifts from ladies of quality; they can ride in carriages, dress splendidly, and outdo kings in the lavishness of their table.[22]

With so much at stake, what's really surprising was that there weren't more holy battles for papal supremacy. When all was said and done, and Damasus was standing victoriously atop the Christian carnage, the street fight between him and his papal rival had caused the deaths of 137 people inside a church basilica on a single day.[23] Ursinus was exiled, and some semblance of Christian order was restored.

***Delivery of the Keys to San Pedro* by Pietro Perugino.**

Although Damasus did many otherwise wonderful things, such as commissioning the most influential Bible ever, the Vulgate, and seeking to protect the church from heresy, within no time he was accused of murder and even adultery—quite a curious indictment for a man who was supposed to be celibate. He dodged these accusations with stealth—it helps to have friends in high places, and Damasus was connected with the Roman cream of the crop. Still, despite his many successes, the Italian bishops never completely warmed to their new boss. Upon asking his fellow bishops for their approval of Ursinus's exile two years later at his birthday party, the bishops replied in unison: "We came together to celebrate a birthday, not to condemn someone without a hearing."[24]

According to contemporary reports, "the ladies of quality…loved Damasus."[25] Turns out this pope had a spiritual gift for feminine fundraising: He quickly earned a reputation for draining the bank accounts of wealthy women for the purpose of building his Christian empire. The pope was so proficient in ear tickling aristocratic women that an edict was actually issued in the year 370 that prohibited ordained church leaders like Damasus from visiting widows or accepting anything from "women to whom they have attached themselves privately under the pretext of religion."[26] The edict was required to be read aloud in churches in Rome to press home the point. Jerome, a client of Damasus's who was making a living from slandering religious men residing in Rome, famously wrote that "Some [clergymen] have devoted a lifetime of effort to the task of learning the names, the households, and the characters of married women."[27] (It's no wonder that Jerome was kicked out of Rome by the religious elite once Pope Damasus, his faithful patron, died.)

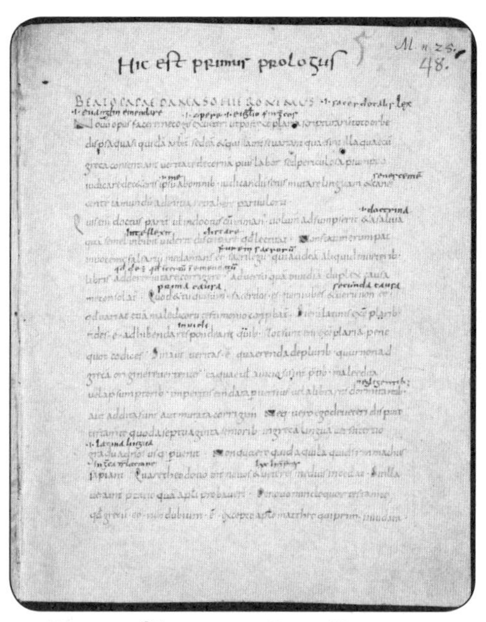

Hic est primus prologus

***Letter of Jerome to Pope Damasus* by Irish monk.**

Not only had religious men like Pope Damasus earned a reputation for ear tickling women of high estate, but he had also earned one for high living. Almost as soon as he assumed office, Damasus went on a building spree that would have Donald Trump green with envy. He built basilicas, completed churches, and garnished martyr shrines with colonnades, pomp, and even poetic verses. As he beautified Rome, he endeared himself to the wealthy pagans of society, making it fashionable and risk-free for them to make a respectable conversion to Christianity without losing their honor, their wealth, and their high-standing in the process. As one classical historian explains:

> Wealthy land-owning families who were attracted to Damasus' 'Roman Christianity' converted in great numbers. To them, the social circuit of martyr commemorations and the pomp and luxury of the liturgical ceremonies invoked the spectacle of lavish pagan religious celebrations.[28]

So lush had Damasus's lifestyle become that the opulence of his personal entertainment surpassed that of the emperor—quite an accomplishment, indeed. It was even said by the residing pagan prefect of Rome that he would gladly convert to Christianity if he could live as fabulously as Damasus did: "Make me bishop of Rome," he pleaded, "and I will become a Christian at once."[29]

NO GREEK MYTHOLOGY IN THIS STORY

Christianity is a beautiful story, to be sure, but it's one studded with the glittering vices of humanity: schism, pride, racism, lust, power, selfishness, violence. The more we attempt to sugarcoat the past or deny that the church needs to spend time in a confessional booth, the more we delude ourselves, send a false message to the world, and set up Christian converts for failure. It's pretty hard to demand perfection from followers of Christ when their leaders can't seem to get things together. Without at all implying that all early Christian leaders were hopeless quacks, God didn't build his kingdom with the precious unalloyed metals buried deep in the rocks and mountains. Nor did God make use of any half-divine, half-human characters from the likes of Greek or Roman mythology. In the early history of Christianity, we will hear nothing of Athena or Hermes. Nor of Artemis or Apollo. As Peter himself adamantly explains in his second letter, "we did not follow cleverly devised myths" (1:16). Instead, we encounter men and women who reached for heaven while staying firmly planted on earth. We encounter sinner-saints who blessed with their right hands and cursed with their left. We encounter broken leaders whose mean-spirited actions routinely spoke louder than their kindhearted words. The highest office in Christianity, the papacy, was filled by men who were just as human as the rest of us. They wore their foibles on their sleeves, and they all led with a limp—just as we do.

ENDNOTES

1 "The Letter of Peter to James and Its Reception," in Bart Ehrman, *After the New Testament: A Reader in Early Christianity* (Oxford: Oxford University Press, 1999), 137.

2 Jerome, *Epistle 12*, quoted in Robert Berchman, *Porphyry Against the Christians* (Leiden, The Netherlands: Brill, 2005), 64.

3 Augustine, *City of God* 19.23, trans. Henry Bettenson (London: Penguin, 1984), 886.

4 Jerome, *Commentary on Galatians*, trans. Andrew Cain (Washington, D.C.: The Catholic University Press of America, 2010), 107.

5 Jerome, *Commentary*, 108.

6 Justin Martyr, "Dialogue with Trypho 11," in *The Fathers of the Church: A New Translation*, vol. 6, *Writings of Saint Justin Martyr*, trans. Thomas Falls (Washington, DC: The Catholic University of America Press, 1977), 164.

7 Eusebius, *The History of the Church* 5.24, trans. G. A. Williamson (London: Penguin, 1989), 173.

8 Pheme Perkins, "Schism and Heresy: Identity, Cracks, and Canyons in Early Christianity," in *The Routledge Companion to Early Christian Thought*, ed. D. Jeffrey Bingham (Oxford and New York: Routledge, 2010), 229.

9 Ibid., 172.

10 Ibid., 172.

11 Eusebius, *The History of the Church* 7.2, 221.

12 James Papandrea, *Novatian of Rome and the Culmination of the Pre-Nicene Orthodoxy* (Eugene, OR: Pickwick Publications, 2012), 135.

13 Novatian, "Letter 2.6," in *The Fathers of the Church: A New Translation*, vol. 67, *Novatian: The Trinity, The Spectacles, Jewish Foods, In Praise of Purity, Letters*, trans. Russell De Simone (Washington, DC: The Catholic University of America Press, 1976), 199.

14 Cyprian, "On the Unity of the Church 6," in *The Fathers of the Church: A New Translation*, vol. 36, *Saint Cyprian: Treatises*, trans. Roy Deferrari (Washington, DC: The Catholic University Press of America, 1958), 100.

15 Cyprian, "Letter 72.1," in *The Fathers of the Church: A New Translation*, vol. 51, *Saint Cyprian: Letters (1-81)*, trans. Rose Bernard Donna (Washington, DC: The Catholic University Press of America, 1981), 265; but following the translation given by Alistair McGrath, "Cyprian of Carthage on Heretical Baptism," in *The Christian Theology Reader* (Oxford: Blackwell, 1997), 291.

16 Cyprian, "Letter 75.25," in 51:312.

17 Geoffrey Willis, *Saint Augustine and the Donatist Controversy* (Eugene, OR: Wipf & Stock, 2005; reprint), 149.

18 Quoted in Christian Hornung, "Siricius and the Rise of the Papacy," in *The Bishop of Rome in Late Antiquity*, ed., Geoffrey Dunn (Surrey: Ashgate, 2015), 66.

19 Hornung, "Siricius and the Rise of the Papacy," in *The Bishop of Rome*, 71 (italics added).

20 Richard McBrien, *Lives of the Popes: The Pontiffs from St. Peter to John Paul II* (New York: HarperSanFrancisco, 2000), 63.

21 Henry Chadwick, *The Early Church* (London: Penguin, 1993; rev.), 160.

22 Quoted in Claudia Rapp, *Holy Bishops in Late Antiquity: The Nature of Christian Leadership in an Age of Transition* (Berkeley, CA: The University of California Press, 2013), 218.

23 John Matthews, "Four Funerals and a Wedding: This World and the Next in Fourth-Century Rome," in *Transformations of Late Antiquity: Essays for Peter Brown*, vol. 2, ed. Philip Rousseau and Emmanuel Papoutsakis (Surrey: Ashgate, 2009), 131.

24 Quoted in McBrien, *Lives of the Popes*, 63.

25 Quoted in Alan Cameron, *The Last Pagans of Rome* (Oxford: Oxford University Press, 2011), 186.

26 *Codex Theodosianus* 16.2.20, quoted in Cameron, *The Last Pagans of Rome*, 186.

27 Jerome, Letter 22.28, quoted in David Hunter, *Marriage, Celibacy and Heresy in Ancient Christianity: The Jovinianist Controversy* (Oxford: Oxford University Press, 2007), 209.

28 Cynthia White, *The Emergence of Christianity: Classical Traditions in Contemporary Perspective* (Minneapolis, MN: Fortress Press, 2011), 110.

29 Jerome, "Against John of Jerusalem 8," quoted in *Christianity in the Later Roman Empire: A Sourcebook*, ed. David Gwynn (London: Bloomsbury Academic, 2015), 113.

30 Novatian, "Letter 1.7," in *The Fathers of the Church: A New Translation*, vol. 67, *Novatian: The Trinity, The Spectacles, Jewish Foods, In Praise of Purity, Letters*, trans. Russell De Simone (Washington, DC: The Catholic University of America Press, 1976), 193–94.

Chapter 3

MARCHING TOWARD DEATH—MARTYRS AND SAINTS

The old man was marching slowly yet happily toward his death. Though the highly respected bishop of Antioch, one of the largest and most important cities in the Roman Empire, Ignatius was chained like a common criminal and accompanied by a band of ten Roman soldiers. "From Syria all the way to Rome," he wrote to the Roman Christians, "I am fighting with wild beasts, on land and sea, by night and day, chained amidst ten leopards...who only get worse when they are well treated." Rather than being swallowed by fear, however, this old bishop was bubbling over with excitement. He was getting closer to Rome, the city where he would be eaten alive by wild animals. "Now at last," his eyes twinkled in holy anticipation of his gruesome death, "I am beginning to be a disciple."

For many nights, Ignatius had been dreaming about the heavenly crown awaiting him after the wild beasts in Rome devoured his earthly head. Rather than complain about the ill treatment he received as a criminal, Ignatius wrote to the churches in Rome for one reason alone: He had heard a dreadful rumor that some well-connected Christians there were seeking to pull some political strings that would keep him out of harm's way. Although Christians today would be overjoyed to hear that they were freed from what promised to be a most excruciating death, Ignatius was none too pleased. He was, in fact, in a huff. He had not volunteered himself to be killed as a martyr just to be freed by an act of clemency. Who would dare stand in the way of his death march? Who would dare rob him of his martyr's crown?

Wasting no time, Ignatius thrust pen to paper and wrote a hasty letter pleading with the Romans to, for heaven's sake, leave him alone and let his body be mangled to bits by ferocious animals. "Let me," he pleaded, "be food for the wild beasts...Better yet, coax the wild beasts, that they may become my tomb and leave nothing of my body behind...Then I will truly be a disciple of Jesus Christ." Restless as a schoolboy anticipating summer vacation, Ignatius continued:

> Fire and cross and battles with wild beasts, mutilation, mangling, wrenching of bones, the hacking of limbs, the crushing of my whole body, cruel tortures of the devil—let these come upon me, only let me reach Jesus Christ![1]

Ignatius, to his heart's delight, lost life and limb in the Coliseum in Rome around the year 107. Now, at long last, he was a true Christian disciple. He was in good company. Like the mighty apostles Peter and Paul, who had likewise spilt their blood in Rome and who had afterward entered the Christian hall of fame, Ignatius had marched toward death and strutted over it like a victorious peacock. With his earthly body mangled and in bits, his soul was now basking in the Almighty presence of God's very light.

A GRAIN OF WHEAT AND A DOOR TO HEAVEN

Although many modern readers of Ignatius wince at the old man's glee in the face of a gruesome death, and one prominent church historian even characterized his actions as "bordering on mania,"[2] Ignatius wrote at a time when physical death for Christ was the pinnacle of piety. Well before Freudian theory urged us to attribute Ignatius's yearning for death to his desire to kill his earthly father, Christians had been willingly giving their lives for their Heavenly Father since the first century. Early Christians patterned their lives after Jesus, whose agonizing death set a model for all those who were willing to "take up their crosses" in order to follow their Master. Didn't Jesus say, for instance, that it's only after a "grain of wheat falls into the earth and dies" that it can then bear "much fruit" (John 12:24)? The earliest Christians grew to accept this idea—and not just because many of them were seasoned farmers. As Ignatius's younger contemporary, Bishop Polycarp, stated in the face of his own martyrdom, "we...love the martyrs as disciples and imitators of the Lord."[3]

***Ignatius of Antioch*. Courtesy of Shakko.**

Many ancient Christians desired to check out of their earthly habitations earlier than scheduled. Life on earth, after all, was simply a rehearsal for an eternal bliss in heaven, and there was no good reason why Christians should delay the ultimate show. Contrary to standards of living in developed countries today, the ancient world was grueling, brief, and rampant with death. As historian Peter Brown wrote about Ignatius's time period:

> Citizens of the Roman Empire at its height, in the second century A.D., were born into the world with an average life expectancy of less than twenty-five years. Death fell savagely on the young. Those who survived childhood remained at risk. Only four out of every hundred men, and fewer women, lived beyond the age of fifty. It was a population 'grazed thin by death.'[4]

Our friend Ignatius, possibly in his seventies, had already cheated death by living as long as he had. Based on the average life expectancy of his day, he had already lived three lives—so what was the point of living a fourth?

Ignatius was not alone in his thinking. With preachers today exhorting us to live everyday like it's Friday, it's hard for us to grasp why early Christians would rather be eaten alive by wild beasts than move to Florida for an early retirement. Constantly keeping in mind how short life expectancies were in the ancient world, Christians marched delightfully towards their deaths for reasons at once biblical and logical as well as macabre and obsessive. We need to delve deeper into their world, however, before we can begin to make sense of their fascination with martyrdom—a Greek-based term that means "witnessing" to one's faith.

FULL-BODY BIBLE READING

Most of us are familiar with the passage encouraging us to sell our possessions and tear out our right eye if it makes us stumble, but few of us have probably ever attempted to follow it in a literal way. Without suggesting that the earliest Christians tore away their limbs in obedience to Scripture, the ancient church generally practiced what we might call a full-body reading of Scripture. That is to say, when they heard Scripture read to them (we have to keep in mind that most early Christians could neither read nor write), they responded in a physical way just as much as a spiritual one.

Consider Jesus's words for us to "cut off" our hand if it is the source of our stumbling or for some of us to "become eunuchs for the kingdom of heaven" (Matt. 19:12). While many of us today read such passages and scratch our heads wondering if we need to get our eyes checked, some early Christians simply took Jesus at his word. It's rumored by an early church historian that one cock-eyed idealist named Origen, a prolific theologian living in the third century in Egypt and Palestine, applied these words in a "literal sense."[5] In an age when chastity was a badge of piety, Origen reportedly had himself castrated to avoid suspicion of sexual impropriety. If any readers find such an act appalling or scandalous, you're in good company. Jesus's disciples did, too. After stating that some people were destined to "become eunuchs for the kingdom of heaven," Jesus responded to the quizzical looks on his disciples' faces by asserting, "Let the one who is able to receive this receive it" (Matt. 19:12).

***Origen*. Courtesy of Serge Lachinov.**

Origen received it. That's one reason many of his writings were later burned and he was condemned at church councils. The church can't have its best theologians taking Scripture too literally. Origen's full-body reading of Scripture, however, is not an isolated example. Living a few generations after Origen in Egypt, a young man named Anthony turned from riches to rags as he sought to fully live out the teachings of Jesus. It's the exact opposite story we hear in contemporary American Christianity, which so often celebrates how God moves Christians from being broke to being blessed—financially, of course. In America, when Christians are in financial straits, we question why God is angry with us. But that's not how many ancient Christians would have thought. According to a prominent fourth-century bishop named Athanasius, upon hearing Jesus's command at church one day to "sell all that you have and give it to the poor" (Matt. 19:21), the Egyptian Anthony "immediately" left the building, gave away his possessions and hundreds of acres of fertile land, only keeping a little money aside for his "sister's sake." However, after hearing the Great Shepherd's order "not [to] be anxious about tomorrow"[6] (Matt. 6:34) as he went back to church, he felt sheepish for keeping some money aside for his sis-

> Although moderns may find fault with Origen's reading of Scripture, he was perhaps the brightest scholar of his generation. A Christian prodigy from the cosmopolitan Greek city of Alexandria, he wrote around a thousand books before dying as a result of physical torture.

ter. He therefore immediately left church, giving the extra money to the poor and entrusting his sister to a convent, while he took up Jesus's cross by crucifying his flesh and eking out the remainder of his earthly existence as a destitute desert father.

For those of us reading this story through a Western and modern lens, we roll our eyes in condescension at Anthony's naïve interpretive tactics. We also take serious fault with Anthony's slapdash decision to surrender his sister's dowry and force her into a calling for which she might not have been resuited. Well before Shakespeare's Hamlet callously ordered Ophelia to "get thee to a nunn'ry," Anthony flung his sister into a convent irrespective of her wishes—or so we assume. Yet Anthony, who knew that life on earth was short and hard, believed it was better for his sister to suffer for a spell in exchange for an everlasting and blissful life in heaven. After all, Paul had urged the Christians in Corinth that it was better for the unmarried to remain single just as he was, for "the time is short" (1 Cor. 7:29). Jesus, however, was much more pointed—and provocative: "If anyone comes to me and does not hate his father and mother, his wife and children, his brothers and sisters—yes, even his own life—he cannot be my disciple" (Luke 14:26). Harboring a holy hatred for both his life and that of his sister's, Anthony sacrificed both for the sake of discipleship. He was willing to stake his fortune on his faith.

Saint Anthony reportedly lived from 251 to 356. Although he certainly wasn't the first monk of the Christian tradition, he is often regarded as the father of monasticism. Through the popularity of Bishop Athanasius of Alexandria's biography of Anthony in the late fourth century, called *Life of Anthony*, Anthony's life set the pattern of monastic behavior.

***The Torment of Saint Anthony* by Michelangelo.**

FOLLOWING THE TRAIL OF BLOOD

Listening to the Bible with the ears of Origen and Anthony, it's not difficult to imagine how full-bodied an interpretation of the following passage from 1 Peter would sound among some in the early church: "For to this you have been called, because Christ also suffered for you, leaving you an example, so that you might follow in his steps" (2:21). In the earliest centuries of the church, these words were not pious platitudes or chicken soup for our souls. They were a death march. To be a Christian was to painfully suffer as Jesus had. It was not a box to check every Sunday after the church's pot-luck dinner. It was not a badge of respectability within a surface-level Christian society. Christianity was about death—first, the death of Christ for one's sins and, then, the death of the self in imitation of Christ. But make no mistake, it was about dying. It's not a coincidence, after all, that one New Testament scholar called the Gospels "passion narratives with extended introductions."[7]

> The early Christians in present-day Iran fully understood the implications of passages like 1 Peter. There, under the Sassanian Dynasty, potentially thousands of Christian martyrs were made in the fourth century alone.

Like a gruesome trail toward suffering, Jesus's drops of blood guided believers toward their own deaths, and it's no surprise that it was during the early church that the "stations of the cross" emerged so that pilgrims to Jerusalem could literally trace the steps of Jesus's path toward a ghastly death. Without a doubt, martyrdom has a holy history in the early church. "In times of persecution," one author mused, "the answer to the question 'What would Jesus do?' is that Jesus would die."[8] That would not likely find its place on many bracelets today. The first Christian martyr, Stephen, had followed the sorrowful way of Jesus, earning a martyr's crown by doing so. Before that, John the Baptist could be regarded as a martyr, as could several figures in the Old Testament and what is called the Old Testament Apocrypha. As for the apostles of Christ, there is a long tradition that every one of them, save John, died as martyrs, some of whose deaths were horrific.

Even Peter, who once denied that he even knew Jesus, redeemed himself by dying a martyr's death in imitation of his Lord. As Peter dictated the words quoted above to his scribe in his old age, he must have visualized the beatings of Jesus and his excruciating death on the cross, knowing that he would soon face death himself. As one account of Peter's death explains, called the *Acts of Peter*, Peter was leaving Rome in haste as a criminal on trumped-on charges of dangerous teaching while he encountered the most unexpected of passers-by:

> And as [Peter] was leaving the city, he saw the Lord entering Rome. And when he saw him, he said: "Lord, where are you going?" And the Lord said to him: "I am going into Rome to be crucified." And Peter said: "Lord, are you being crucified again?" He said: "Yes, Peter, I am being crucified again." And Peter came to himself. And having seen the Lord ascend into heaven, he returned to Rome, rejoicing and glorifying the Lord. He said: "I will be crucified."[9]

Peter joyfully followed the bloody footsteps of Jesus into Rome, was crucified, and finally got to live out what Jesus has taught him about taking up his cross. As Peter wrote before his death, "whoever has suffered in the flesh has finished with sin" (1 Peter 4:1).

But Peter was not the only one who overcame sin. His death was part of a larger, but still localized, persecution of Christians in the mid-60s that also took the life of the apostle Paul. After a run-away fire in the city of Rome damaged many of the districts, it was Christians who became the scapegoat for Emperor Nero, a man

***The Crucifixion of Saint Peter* by Caravaggio.**

***Nero's Torches* by Henryk Siemiradzki.**

Although some believe that Christians in Rome hid in the catacombs to escape persecution, that probably never happened. The catacombs were places of burial. Dark and dank, they were a series of corridors where small rooms and niches were carved out to house the remains of the Christian deceased. Anyone with an oil lamp and a high threshold for small spaces and strong smells was free to descend into the catacombs.

who was as insidious as he was inventive. This emperor reportedly killed hundreds of Christians in Rome—some eaten by wild dogs, some nailed to crosses, and some used as human torches to light the imperial gardens. So great was the torture of Christians that a Roman historian named Tacitus, a man who was no friend to the church, remarked that although these Christians "deserved extreme and exemplary punishment, there arose a feeling of compassion"[10] among the Roman populace.

This sense of compassion did not last. Although Romans didn't hunt down Christians except on very rare occasions, martyrdom crowned the life of the most faithful Christians in the early church. With the martyrdoms of so many prominent Christians in the first century, it didn't take long before a sort of religious cult developed around those willing—whether coerced or volunteered—to give their lives for their faith. "Already by the end of the second century," writes historian Robin Young, "Christians cherished their martyrs as saints, or 'holy ones.'"[11] Christians formed holy huddles around the graves of the blessed martyrs as a form of veneration on their "birth dates," that is, the days these men and women lost life and limb for Christ.

Like Moses at the burning bush, the place on which these devotees were standing was sacred. It was holy ground. The shrines of the martyrs were intimately accessible—open to women and men, old and young, priest and pauper. Like an aging bottle of wine properly stored in a damp cellar, the relics of the martyrs became more potent over time, capable of curing sicknesses, undoing demonic possession, and answering prayers like no bottle of Cabernet Sauvignon ever did. Martyrdom, after all, earned the person a direct ticket to heaven—with an earthly fan club rivaling that of any modern celebrity. As one Christian author of the turn of the third century wrote, "The only key that unlocks the gates of Paradise is your own blood."[12] "No, thanks," many moderns might reply, "we'll find another entrance."

MASOCHISM OR MARTYRDOM? SUICIDE OR SANCTITY?

In the context of such bloody rhetoric, it's not surprising that some scholars have regarded those who died for Christ as masochists rather than martyrs. Lyford Edwards, one of the pioneers of the discipline of sociology, wrote that "The masochistic phenomena are the most remarkable characteristic of the early martyrdoms."[13] Masochistic or not, historian

Lacey Smith considered martyrdom "abnormal behavior"—more indicative of a "self-destructive and masochistic urge" than it was a sane and sacred piety. Though these authors are perhaps wide of the mark when it comes to understanding early Christian martyrdom, they are certainly correct to suggest that early Christianity's "appetite for death…could get out of hand."[14] What are we to make of Christians who threw themselves into harm's way unprovoked? Were they martyrs or simply mad?

In his book *Radical Martyrdom and Cosmic Conflict in Early Christianity*, author Paul Middleton addresses "those Christians who so desired death, that they intentionally sought out arrest and martyrdom."[15] Such "radical" Christians straddled the border of sanctity and suicide. We witness this spectrum of sanctity-suicide in a fourth-century report about a group of martyr-hungry Christians called the "mountaineers." "Because they love the name martyr," the ancient document candidly stated, "they kill themselves." Continuing on:

> After they have uttered a prayer, they commit suicide by throwing themselves off a height, by self-immolation, or by the sword. That is, by asking other persons to kill them. They do this so that by departing from this life violently, they will acquire the name of martyrs.[16]

As aghast as this makes many modern readers feel who associate martyrdom-suicide with Muslim extremism, early Christians were very familiar with this practice. In the late second century, it was reported that a woman named Agathonike, watching innocently from the sidelines as two Christian clerics were being burned at the stake, could not suppress her yearning to be burned alive. Throwing caution to the wind—and her clothes to the ground—she jumped headlong into the swelling fire, shouting "Here is the meal that has been prepared for me: I must partake and eat of this glorious meal."[17] Partake of it she did. But her young son was to go hungry, for she left him alone to watch his mother burn to death despite the protestations of the bystanders. The story, far from condemning Agathonike's decision to kill herself and leave her son an orphan, valorized her death by self-sacrifice:

> And she thus gave up her spirit and died together with the saints. And the Christians secretly collected their remains and protected them for the glory of Christ and the praise of his martyrs.[18]

Writing around the year 250, the soon-to-be-martyred Novatian of Rome exclaimed: "What could be more glorious than to confess Christ, the Son of God, amid the most diverse and most exquisite tortures of a cruel, secular power? The body is racked, lacerated, stripped of its flesh, but the spirit, even though it is leaving the body, still remains free."[30]

With such approval of what many would regard as selfishness at best and suicide at worst, it's no wonder that voluntary martyrdom continued for centuries. It was an excruciating, yet express, entrance into heaven. Why delay the inevitable? In the early fourth century, a man named Euplus rushed to the office of the prefect in his city. Yelling for the prefect to come out, he begged for death: "I want to die; I am a Christian." Had Euplus not stormed the prefect's office like a fanatic on a date with death, he unquestionably would have lived on in peace and not been bothered at all. But just like the persistent widow in the Gospel of Luke who pestered the judge for a positive verdict, Euplus harassed the prefect so vigorously that his prayer was ultimately answered. He was tortured for his refusal to sacrifice to the Roman gods, and thereby "received the crown of orthodox belief."[19] Despite the fact that he volunteered himself for death like a military recruit looking for a war during a time of peace, he was accorded the honor of a martyr—a true soldier for Christ. But if we measure such actions "by modern standards," many would conclude "martyrs" like this man were "suicidal."[20]

MAY SUCH A LOT BE YOURS!

If we perused the shelves of Christian bookstores today, we would be wont to find a book that encouraged us to die. On the contrary, our most popular Christian books promise us not only that promotion we've always coveted but an unsurpassed medical and dental plan with six weeks of paid vacation. We can have Jesus—and health, and wealth, and great sex. God is that good—all the time.

This type of book would not have sold many copies in the early church. And that's not because fewer than ten percent of the population could read. Always keeping in mind, life expectancies were at least three times shorter than today, the end of the world was expected to occur any moment, and suffering and death were understood to be central features of the biblical story and of life in general, we suspect just the opposite type of book to be commended in the ancient world. Writing in the third century in Africa, authors Tertullian and Origen both composed books on martyrdom. They had cut their teeth on stories of Christian bloodshed, and now, as mature thinkers, had the theology to sustain their brazen arguments that dying for one's faith was not only an honor but a duty. That's right—a duty. Their books are an all-out assault on much of what parades about in our bookstores as "Christian living." "Christian dying," they might say—that's the real Christian life.

In Origen's *Exhortation to Martyrdom*, he reminded Christians of the holy compact they had made with God:

> We must understand that we have accepted what are called the covenants of God as agreements we have made with Him when we undertook to live the Christian life. And among our agreements with God was the entire citizenship of the gospel, which says, 'If anyone would come after me, let him deny himself and take up his cross and follow me. For whoever would save his

> soul would lose it, and whoever loses his soul for my sake will save it' (Mt. 16:24-25)...If we wish to save our soul in order to get it back better than a soul, let us lose it by our martyrdom...May such a lot be yours.[21]

For Origen, martyrdom was a benefit of heavenly citizenship. To reject martyrdom, if that was one's "lot," was to reject Christ. In the book, Origen unleashed an arsenal of biblical texts, interpreted within a context of imminent death, urging the believer to consider martyrdom as the crown of one's holy achievement on earth. It's a book that celebrates the heaping of coals over one's head for the sake of righteousness, for, as Jesus said, "Blessed are those who are persecuted" (Matt. 5:10).

Writing a generation before Origen, Tertullian presented a distressing yet vigorous exhortation to those dying for their faith. Tertullian is perhaps most famous for a four-word statement he once uttered: *semen est sanguis Christianorum*[22]—which bleeds over into English translation in more than double the amount of words, "the blood of Christian martyrs is the seed of the Church." Egging on secular rulers, this Latin penman heckled his opponents with spellbinding sarcasm, "Crucify, torture, condemn, grind us all to powder if you can...the more you mow us down, the thicker we rise."[23] Tertullian may well have been right. Onlookers, even within the violent culture of the Roman Empire who thought nothing of watching wild animals maul gladiators for the sake of entertainment, pitied some of the Christians who were mowed down like grass on a summer's day. In a paradox reminiscent of Paul's dictum, "when I am weak, then I am strong" (2 Cor. 12:10), the uprooting of Christians by death only led to the flowering of their faith. It was an affront to Roman supremacy.

Tertullian, like Origen after him, compared the life of the martyr to that of a sporting contest in which the Holy Spirit was the believer's trainer who provides "a harsher treatment [so] that your strength may be increased" when the time comes for the martyr's death in the arena.[24] Writing about a decade letter to Christians who were fleeing during persecution in a book called *Flight in the Time of Persecution*, Tertullian made the argument that "God is the author of persecution,"[25] and that to flee from persecution was to turn one's back on God. Applying John's saying that Jesus "laid down his life for us" (1 John 3:16), Tertullian maintained that we must do the same for Jesus. Countering the worldly wisdom that it is better to fly from persecution and live another day, Tertullian asked instead, "Is it such a terrible thing to die?" After all, he calmly reasoned, we each have to die someday, so wouldn't it be better to go ahead and die now for Christ? "Personally," he explained, "I would rather be an object of pity [for dying for my faith] than of shame [for fleeing when times are tough]."[26]

Although the average Christian didn't drink from the fountains of Origen and Tertullian, these two thinkers distilled much of the more professionalized theology about martyrdom in the early church. Rather than shirk back from death, it was a Christian's divine calling, they believed, to em-

***Clement of Alexandria* by André Thévet.**

brace suffering and proceed headlong into harm's way. As a second-century theologian named Clement of Alexandria reasoned, we are "on the boundary between a mortal and an immortal nature."[27] It is death that directs us into the realm of immortality, so why live longer than necessary in the world of mortality? Although the numbers of Christian martyrs in the Roman Empire will never be known with any precision, it's possible that tens of thousands died a martyr's death—whether self-motivated or not. Tens of thousands more died in Iran and beyond the empire.

Many more Christians, however, risked neither hide nor hair for their faith. When bursts of persecutions occurred during the first, second, and third centuries, they were content to flee, bribe, or lie in order to avoid persecution or, God forbid, death. Perhaps they were the Thomas Jeffersons of their age, who cut out all of the verses in the Gospels that were an affront to their sensibilities. Whatever the case, these less-than-enthusiastic Christians notwithstanding, the ideal was to face persecution head-on in imitation of Jesus and the disciples—and the unbroken chain of holy martyrs that included the likes of Ignatius, Polycarp, Justin Martyr, the Scillitan Martyrs, Perpetua and Felicity, Fabian, and Agnes.

THOSE LESS THAN DO-GOODER CHRISTIANS

But all for nothing. According to New Testament scholar Candida Moss, early Christians "invented" the notion of persecution. In her book, *The Myth of Persecution*, she maintains that "There is a difference between persecution and prosecution."[28] For far too long, she bemoans, historians have bewailed the cruel treatment of Christians within the Roman Empire, mistaking being targeted for one's beliefs ("persecution") for violating a known public law ("prosecution"). Despite the alluring alliteration, the argument is flawed. There's simply no way to disentangle religion from politics in the ancient world. Besides, we have far too many examples, from Christians and non-Christians alike, leading us to conclude that persecution, sporadic as it was, was not an invention. Prosecutions or persecutions, there were specific times in the Roman Empire when Christians were violently pursued. For instance, we have ample testimony that this occurred under the authority of Emperors Nero (64), Decius (250), Valerian (257–258), Diocletian (303–305), and Maximinus Daia (311–313).

Granted, most Christians did not die from either persecution or prosecution in the early church. But still, many did—and many more were nurtured spiritually by the martyr stories of those who gave their lives for the faith—even if such stories spread orally before being written down. Whether a real threat or imagined, Christians believed themselves to be targets of opposition. The Romans, after all, had many reasons to dislike them, not least because they were seen as subversive, atheistic, superstitious, incestuous, cannibalistic, anti-military, and secretive. If we know anything from the ancient world, it's that the Romans were willing to do whatever it took to gain victory against their enemies, whether inside their borders or outside. Although "Romans were not in the business of marking martyrs,"[29] they were in the business of violently maintaining order and doing whatever it took to remain on top. If that meant crushing a new political-religious movement, so be it.

The greatest persecution in the Roman Empire was the Diocletian Persecution, often known as the Great Persecution. It targeted Christian bishops, confiscated and burnt copies of the Scriptures, and destroyed churches.

A MARTYR NO MORE

But then everything changed. The well of persecution, and even prosecution, dried up. In the early fourth century, Emperor Constantine made Christianity legal—even prestigious. Issuing the Edict of Milan in the year 313 with his co-emperor Licinius, he eased tension against the Christian religion. Constantine himself was baptized into the church shortly before his death, blazing a religious trail for Roman emperors to follow for centuries to come. And just like that, the Roman Empire became the incubator of the church. A frightening thought, to be sure. By the end of the fourth century, pagan worship was prohibited and churches were budding forth like flowers in the springtime. No more death for Christ—at least not in the Roman Empire. The Age of the Martyrs had ended. The Age of Faith had begun. Apparently, the quota of martyr's crowns had been reached. The only acceptable sacrifices now were those performed by male priests during Mass, and the only blood spilled was the turning of wine into Christ's blood at the altar among lawfully ordained and state-supported Christian priests. This change was as sudden as it was significant.

ENDNOTES

1 Ignatius, "The Letter to the Romans," in *The Apostolic Fathers*, 2nd ed., ed. Michael Holmes (Grand Rapids, MI: Baker, 1989), 103–104.

2 William Frend, *Martyrdom and Persecution in the Early Church: A Study of Conflict from the Maccabees to Donatus* (Eugene, OR: Wipf & Stock, 2014), 198.

3 "The Martyrdom of Polycarp," in *Ignatius of Antioch and Polycarp: A New Translation and Theological Commentary*, trans. Kenneth Howell (Zanesville, OH: CHResources, 2009), 171

4 Peter Brown, *The Body and Society: Men, Women, and Sexual Renunciation in Early Christianity* (New York: Columbia University Press, 1988), 6.

5 Eusebius, the *History of the Church* 6.8 (London: Penguin, 1989), 186.

6 Athanasius, *Life of Anthony* 1–3.

7 Martin Kahler, *The So-Called Historical Jesus and the Historic, Biblical Christ*, trans. Carl Braaten (Philadelphia: Fortress, 1964), 80.

8 Candida Moss, *The Myth of Persecution: How Early Christians Invented a Story of Martyrdom* (New York: HarperOne, 2013), 5.

9 *Acts of Peter* 35.

10 Tacitus, *Annals* 15.44.

11 Robin Darling, "Martyrdom as Exaltation," in *Late Ancient Christianity*, ed. Virginia Burrus (Minneapolis, MN: Fortress Press, 2010), 71.

12 Tertullian, *On the Soul* 55.4–5, vol. 10, *The Fathers of the Church: Tertullian Apologetical Works and Minucius Felix Octavius*, trans. Rudolph Arbesmann (Washington, DC: Catholic University Press of America, 1950), 300.

13 Lyford Edwards, *The Transformation of Early Christianity from an Eschatological to a Social Movement* (Menasha, WI: George Banta, 1919), 21.

14 Lacey Baldwin Smith, *Fools, Martyrs, Traitors: The Story of Martyrdom in the Western World* (New York: Alfred Knopf, 1997), 62.

15 Paul Middleton, *Radical Martyrdom and Cosmic Conflict in Early Christianity* (London and New York: T&T Clark, 2006), 1.

16 "Indiculus de Haeresibus," quoted in, Brent Shaw, "Bad Boys: Circumcellions and Fictive Violence," in *Violence in Late Antiquity: Perceptions and Practices*, ed. Harold Drake (Aldershot and Burlington, VT: Ashgate, 2006), 182.

17 Robert Rainy, *The Ancient Catholic Church: From the Accession of Trajan to the Fourth General Council* (New York: Charles Scribner's Sons, 1902), 49.

18 Quoted in Middleton, *Radical Martyrdom*, 33.

19 Quoted in Middleton, *Radical Martyrdom*, 30.

20 Moss, *The Myth of Persecution*, 196.

21 Origen, "Exhortation to Martyrdom," in *Origen: An Exhortation to Martyrdom, Prayer, and Select Works*, trans. Rowan Greer (New York, Ramsey, and Toronto: Paulist Press, 1979), 49, 51.

22 Tertullian, *Apologeticum* 50, Patrologia Latina 1:535. Edited by J.-P. Migne. 217 vols. (Paris, 1844–1863).

23 Tertullian, *Apologeticum* 50 [13].

24 Tertullian, "To the Martyrs," in *Disciplinary, Moral and Ascetical Works*, vol. 40, *The Fathers of the Church* (New York: Fathers of the Church, Inc., 1959), 20, 23.

25 Tertullian, "Flight in Times of Persecution," in *Disciplinary, Moral and Ascetical Works*, 282.

26 Tertullian, "Flight," in *Disciplinary, Moral and Ascetical Works*, 295.

27 Clement of Alexandria, "Stromateis," in *Stromateis: Books One to Three*, vol. 85, *The Fathers of the Church* (Washington, DC: The Catholic University of America Press, 1991), 212.

28 Moss, *The Myth of Persecution*, 14.

29 George Kalantzis, *Caesar and the Lamb: Early Christian Attitudes on War and Military Service* (Eugene, OR: Cascade Books, 2012), 26.

30 Novatian, "Letter 2.3," in *The Fathers of the Church: A New Translation*, vol. 67, *Novatian: The Trinity, The Spectacles, Jewish Foods, In Praise of Purity, Letters*, trans. Russell De Simone (Washington, DC: The Catholic University of America Press, 1976), 196–97.

Chapter 4

GOING TO CHURCH—FAITH AND PRACTICE

Writing to his beloved sister, he was downright giddy with excitement. In the summer of 386, after seven years of building a church bearing his own name, Bishop Ambrose of Milan had struck gold—or, at least, the Christian equivalent. Finding it impossible to compose himself in light of such a divine discovery, Ambrose blurted out in the opening line of his letter, "we have found martyrs"![1] By this time in the history of Christianity, martyrs had attained something slightly short of rock-star status. They were the idols of their age. Although we like to envision early Christians in a holy huddle around their Bibles singing a song by Chris Tomlin, or at least a hymn written by Charles Wesley, they were more likely to be found offering a prayer to a dead saint in the middle of a cemetery. Such deceased saints, after all, had a proven track record of interceding for the living, healing the sick, and even resurrecting the dead—de-

Relics of Ambrose, Gervasius, and Protasius in Milan. Courtesy of BáthoryPéter.

spite, quite remarkably, being dead themselves. By the late fourth century, martyrs could no longer be made in the Roman Empire, but there were enough of their relics to go around—or at least enough religious hawkers willing to manufacture them. These were the booming years of church architecture. Christianity was now not only patroned by emperors but fashionable among the rich and famous, and a church was not really a church unless it possessed the relics of a holy dead person.

Ambrose of Milan, though not the first to transfer the remains of dead saints from cemeteries to churches, popularized this practice. In 386, he led a sacred search party into the outskirts of town after his parishioners requested some holy dead people to furnish their city's new church with religious digs. Strangely, or should we say providentially, Ambrose found some dead saints in no time. Augustine, a disciple of Ambrose living in Milan at this time before becoming bishop of Hippo, confirmed Ambrose's miracle of finding the bones of saints at a cemetery outside of the city. "These bodies had been lost," Augustine reported, "but their hiding-place was revealed in a dream to Ambrose."[2] After finding some bona fide holy relics, Ambrose oozed with excitement: "All the bones," he continued in his letter to his sister "were intact. There was abundance of blood."[3] God's approval of the holy expedition was evidenced when a blind man gained sight after rubbing a cloth on the casket carting the bloodied remains before then rubbing it on his eyes. Centuries before DNA would become a household term, some unlucky victims of demonic possession verified that these decapitated corpses were sacred, the remains of which Ambrose promptly tossed on a wagon and wheeled to church. It was just another day of worship among early Christians.

> As Christianity became more respectable in the Roman Empire, so, too, did the bishops. From the fourth century onward, there was a rise in bishops of senatorial aristocracy like Ambrose of Milan. Because of his wealth and status, Ambrose was fast-tracked to the highest office in Northern Italy. Within the time span of a mere week, he was baptized, ordained, and consecrated as bishop! He had no theological training, but took to his new position with unparalleled zeal.

NOT YOUR MOMMA'S CHURCH

The religious fanfare accompanying Ambrose's discovery of the decapitated saints Protasius and Gervasius sheds light on how many early Christians expressed their faith. Although it's a constant temptation to fashion ancient Christians in our own images as American evangelicals or mainline Protestants, they were nothing of the sort. Early Christian worship was a down-to-earth experience that was sometimes as strange as it was solemn. As historian Andrew McGowan confirms, "The history of early Christian worship [is] not a serene tour through idealized house churches full of believers 'of one heart and soul.'"[4] On the contrary, worship was less domesticated than we care to admit. There was incense to smell, icons to venerate, relics to adore, cemeteries to visit, demons to exorcise, shrines to make pilgrimage to, Christ's body to ingest, feast days to celebrate, processions to watch, cheeks to kiss, signs of the cross to make, a bishop's hands to touch, a priest to confess one's sins to—a sacred space in which to find worship with the communion of the saints, living or dead. Here's what there was not. There were no Bibles to carry to church, no church nativities on the front lawn, and no pews to park one's derriere. These, as familiar as they might be to us, were medieval inventions. Portable Bibles, pews, and nativities didn't emerge until the thirteenth century. And as for church bulletins, worship bands, and fair-trade coffee—try the twentieth century. Truth is, the way early Christians worshiped was like night and day compared to how many do so now.

DINING WITH THE DEAD

We see this most starkly in early Christian devotion to dead people. While many contemporary Christians get the creeps when visiting cemeteries or when in the presence of the departed, early churches wouldn't dream of constructing a church without the holy remains of a dead saint tucked away near the altar. In a society that highly valued both communal eating and honoring the deceased, it should come as no surprise that Christians took to eating with dead saints by the second century. Archaeologists have discovered images of ancient Christians eating with the holy departed, countless religious artifacts housed in cemeteries such as tables, and whole churches and shrines constructed over saints' tombs.

Well before modern churches began the practice of having a summer worship service at the community park, early Christians were erecting picnic tables over gravesites and eating with their favorite dead saints as expressions of faith. Augustine's mother, Monica, a pious Catholic who prayed her son into the kingdom, regularly dined with the dead. This was fairly common among North African Christians. A prominent bishop there once proudly stated: "We offer Sacrifices for [dead saints] always...as often as we celebrate the passions and [birth]days of the martyrs."[5] On the anniversary of a martyr's death, pious Christians would march to the martyr's tomb, have

> Upon the martyrdom of Bishop Polycarp of Smyrna, in the 160s, his flock "took his bones that were more precious than fine jewels and more refined than gold. We put them in a suitable place. Then the Lord granted us who gathered in gladness and joy...to celebrate the birthday of his martyrdom."[37]

supper with the deceased saint, offer prayers, sing a song, and end the pious party by asking for a favor. Occasionally, "there were even dances."[6]

NOT SO FAST

But devotion to the dead was not amusing to everyone. The fourth-century emperor Julian mercilessly mocked Christian practices that encouraged them to worship God among the dead of this world. In his book *Against the Galileans*, he scoffed: "You Christians have filled the whole world with tombs and sepulchers, and yet in your scriptures it is nowhere said that you must grovel among tombs and pay them honour."[7] Perhaps he had a point. A pagan critic named Eunapius was equally horrified at the conduct of Christians: "For they collected the bones and skulls of criminals who had been put to death for numerous crimes...made them out to be gods, and thought that they became better by defiling themselves at their graves."[8] Even Theodosius, a devout *Christian* emperor in the late fourth century, was appalled at this type of Christian behavior. As historian Charles Freeman explains, Theodosius rained on his bishop's parade: "In the same year [Bishop Ambrose transferred the remains of his martyrs], Theodosius issued a law forbidding corpses to be brought for burial within city walls."[9] Not only was this practice of transferring long since dead people into town just plain weird, Theodosius might have mused, it was a threat to public health—who knows what these diseased corpses could transmit to fawning devotees as they lavished their lips over human remains.

> Julian was emperor from 361 to 363. Over the course of his short tenure as emperor, he attempted to eradicate Christianity, revive paganism, and even enliven Judaism by rebuilding the Jewish temple.

KISSING CHRISTIANS

As awkward as it makes many Christians feel today, kissing the remains of the dead was a regular feature of Christian affection. Although some authorities attempted to crack down on the practice, many others regarded it as an acceptable, and even advantageous, way to worship. As historian Peter Brown explains:

> The rise of the Christian cult of saints took place in the great cemeteries that lay outside the cities of the Roman world: and, as for the handling of dead bodies, the Christian cult of saints rapidly came to involve the digging up, the moving, the dismemberment—quite apart from much *avid touching and kissing—of the bones of the dead*, and, frequently, the placing of these in areas from which the dead had once been excluded.[10]

Stories of Christians kissing relics abound in ancient literature. Around the year 300, for example, a Spanish noblewoman living in North Africa made it a habit of kissing the bone of a martyr before taking the Eucharist as a way to heighten her experience.[11] Even the great Augustine ached to touch dead saints with his lips: "we want to embrace and kiss their torn limbs."[12] We shouldn't be surprised at the kissing that took place among early Christians. Kissing, lest we forget, was commanded by both Peter and Paul in their epistles. It was a biblical mandate, divinely directed by the two most prominent church leaders in the history of the Christian religion. Though many churches today lamely interpret biblical injunctions "to greet one another with a holy kiss" as invitations to offer a feeble handshake, or a lackluster pat on the back to parishioners on Sunday mornings, early Christians obeyed these commandments by literally kissing each other on the mouth. Such kissing was, after all, was directly ordered on five separate occasions in the New Testament (Rom. 16:16; 1 Cor. 16:20; 2 Cor. 13:2; 1 Thess. 5:26; 1 Peter 5:14).

In fact, kissing living members of the body of Christ was a central feature of Christianity. As historian Michael Penn explains in his book *Kissing Christians*, "the kiss was one of the most prevalent features of early Christianity...Christians kissed each other during prayer, Eucharist, baptism, and ordination and in connection with greeting, funerals, monastic vows, martyrdom, and penitential practices."[13] In a word, kissing was the currency of devotion. For the early Christian author Tertullian, saying a prayer without offering a kiss was like trying to watch television without plugging it in. As he wrote in a book to his wife, "What prayer is complete if it is divorced from the holy kiss?"[14] Despite this relationship between smooching and the sacred, there was a dark side to Christian kissing. While Tertullian acknowledged that pagan men did not approve of their Christian wives attending church services since they would be urged to "meet any one of the brethren to exchange the kiss,"[15] his contemporary Clement of Alexandria recognized that "the unrestrained use of the kiss" had caused "shameful suspicions and slanders." That's why he urged closed-mouth kissing at church rather than the open-mouthed kissing that "inject[s] the poison of licentiousness."[16] Athenagoras of Athens, another second-century Christian writer, agreed. Knowing that discretion is the better part of valor, Athenagoras subscribed to a one-kiss policy: "If any one kiss[es] a second time because it has given him pleasure, [he sins].'"[17]

With so many open mouths lining the halls of church assemblies, Christian kissing had to be regulated. Only one closed-mouth—and ideally, hurried and ill-liked—holy kiss per person was acceptable per service. Repeat kissing was grounds for suspicion. With a surge of sexual rumors about Christians circulating among the wider public, leaders gradually limited holy kissing to relics, artifacts, and baptized believers of the same tradition—and then ultimately to baptized people of the same gender and baptized people of the same rank (clergy with clergy and laity with laity). Apparently too much kissing was bad for the soul. As for unbelievers and heretical Christians, they would have to find pagans lips to kiss if they wanted a smooch—Christian lips were off limits. In fact, even catechumens, those who had yet to be baptized but who identified as Christians, were denied the lips of the baptized since "their kiss," the *Apostolic Tradition* explains, "[was] not yet pure."[18]

SEPARATING THE KISSERS FROM THE NON-KISSERS

It's not a coincidence that preserving the purity of the faith was part and parcel of early Christianity. The mysteries of the faith had to be protected from the uninitiated. It was only *after* the newly initiated were physically baptized—that is, after their bodies were disrobed, clothed in Christ, and purified—that they were allowed to freely, but not unreservedly, kiss fellow baptized Christians on the mouth. In this way, baptism became the great boundary marker separating the kissers from the non-kissers, the Christians from the non-Christians. No baptism, no kissing—it was that simple.

The association of holy baptism with holy kissing was ancient, though it was not necessarily easy to regulate. Prior to urging kissing among believers, the New Testament authors commanded water baptism as the mark of the faithful. The actual manner of baptism, believe it or not, was less important than we might think among ancient Christians. Although the later history of Christianity is rife with debates on how to baptize, who to baptize, when to baptize, and where to baptize, early Christians took a more moderate approach. The earliest book of church order, written when the apostle John was still alive, sanctioned any number of ways for Christians to baptize:

> Baptize in the name of the Father and of the Son and of the Holy Spirit. Baptize in running water, but if you have no running water, then baptize in some other water. Baptize in cold water, but if you do not have cold water, then use warm water. If you do not have a place with water, then pour water on the head.[19]

The focus of this early document, commonly called the *Didache*, was pragmatism. It's as if the writer was saying, "all things the same, do it this way; if you can't do it this way, do it that way; if you can't do it that way, find another way." The *Apostolic Tradition* was equally indifferent: "use whatever water you can find." Even better, our friend Tertullian was indignant with apathy when it came to the method of baptism: "it makes no matter whether one is washed in the sea or in a puddle, a river or a foundation, a pond or a tub."[20] Although it would have made for much less entertaining history, it probably would have done subsequent Christians a lot of good if they would have simply adopted Tertullian's approach—though baptizing "in a puddle" would surely have been a dirty, if not tricky, enterprise.

Farwell of Saints Peter and Paul
by Alonzo Rodriguez. Courtesy of I, Sailko.

Water source notwithstanding, baptism was fundamental to early Christian faith. Writing in the second half of the second century, Justin Martyr wrote the following about baptism in his book *First Apology*:

> As many as are persuaded and believe that the things we teach and say are true, and undertake to live accordingly, are instructed to pray and ask God with fasting for the remission of their past sins, while we pray and fast with them. Then they are brought by us where there is water, and are born again

> in the same manner of rebirth by which we ourselves were born again, for they then receive washing in water in the name of God the Father and Master of All, and of our Savior, Jesus Christ, and of the Holy Spirit. For Christ also said, 'Except you are born again, you will not enter into the Kingdom of heaven.'[21]

Referred to as baptismal regeneration, early Christians like Justin Martyr believed that spiritual birth, or salvation, occurred the moment a person was baptized. Baptism by water was what actually marked out, in truth "made," someone a Christian. Stated differently, water was the mechanism God used to regenerate a person through the conveyance of the Holy Spirit. As a third-century antipope explained, "It is the Holy Spirit who effects with water the second birth."[22] However we decide to phrase it, spiritual birth and physical baptism were the two sides of the coin of salvation.

> Writing in the middle of the fourth century, Bishop Hilary of Poitiers penned in his commentary on the Gospel of Matthew: Like the baptism of Christ, "we should likewise know that following the waters of baptism, the Holy Spirit comes upon us from the gates of heaven, imbuing us with the anointing of heavenly glory. We become the sons of God."[38]

This was nothing new. According to the book of Acts, the apostle Peter once preached, "Repent, and be baptized every one of you in the name of Jesus Christ *so that your sins may be forgiven; and you will receive the gift of the Holy Spirit*." A literal reading of this passage led early Christians to believe that the act of water baptism expunged one's sins and also filled a person with the Holy Spirit. The passage was read like a simple math equation: Water baptism equals forgiveness of sins plus reception of the Spirit. This is the reverse of how many evangelicals understand the sacrament of water: first being born again spiritually, then physical baptism as an outward sign of an inward reality. The Gospel of Mark says it this way: "The one who believes *and is baptized* will be saved; but the one who does not believe [*and is not baptized*] will be condemned." The First Letter of Peter was even more direct: "baptism…saves you" (3:21).

BAPTISM IN THE NUDE

Although many contemporary churches would reject the doctrine of baptismal regeneration as taught by early Christians, hardly any would have the temerity to duplicate the manner in which early Christian baptized. If they did so, they would invite not only a whopping lawsuit but a sexual scandal that the media would run to like lions in sight of a lame gazelle. Here's why: According to many ancient church documents, all of the baptismal candidates—whether child, man, or woman—were required to "remove their clothing" before entering the water.[23] That's right—candidates were baptized completely naked, ideally after being scrubbed down by an attendant and before being swarmed with dozens of kisses from fellow believers.

Writing about baptism in the late fourth century, the bishop of Jerusalem compared the nakedness of baptismal candidates—"in the sight of all," no less—to the imitation of Christ, "who was stripped naked on the cross." While nude, the bishop reports, the candidates were slathered in oil "from the very hairs of [their] head to [their] feet" by a designated Christian before (or sometimes after) taking a plunge into the water.[24] According to the *Apostolic Tradition*, the priest may also have stood stark naked beside the stripped catechumen—a daring, if not highly imprudent, practice if there ever was one.[25] "Standing naked and dripping with oil," early historian David Hunter writes, "one by one the [baptismal] candidates faced west and heard the bishop ask two questions: 'Do you renounce the devil and his works?'...'Do you renounce the world and its pleasures?'"[26] After responding affirmatively and then facing east to recite a creed and continue in the ritual, kisses of peace and hugs of holiness were possibly allowed before a white tunic was placed on the wet, oily, and exposed body of the newly baptized Christian. As a fifth-century document states:

> Like a newborn from the womb he gazes from the water, but instead of [receiving] garments, the priest receives him and embraces him. He resembles a newborn when he is raised from the water and like a newborn everyone embraces and kisses him.[27]

With so much kissing, smearing, embracing, and nakedness going on, it's no wonder that early Christian services were frequently the butt of pagan jokes. Still, the practice continued for several centuries. Nude baptism, in fact, is abundantly represented in early Christian art. For whatever we may think of early Christians, they weren't prudes. Nude baptismal scenes from the Roman catacombs are our earliest depictions of this bedrock Christian practice. In general, catacomb paintings depict a nude child standing in water next to a taller and clad male, who often has his right hand over the younger person's head. Even Jesus is depicted as a naked infant being baptized by the larger, and clothed, John the Baptist, in this artwork. Why did those undergoing baptism do so without clothing? There were actually numerous reasons, explains early Christian historian of art Robin Jensen, one of which was to symbolize "the way children are born from their mother's wombs."[28] Like newborn babies naked and innocent to the world, those undergoing baptism had their sins wiped away and were restarting life as if they were re-exiting their mother's womb. So apparent was this symbolism that some fifth- and sixth-century baptismal fonts in North Africa were actually constructed in the shape of a woman's vulva.

MYSTERY OF MYSTERIES

It was only after a catechumen was baptized—and then kissed and clothed, of course—that he or she was permitted to take part in the greatest mystery of the church. Stated differently, the most sacred aspect of early Christian services was not the homily the priest preached, the prayer the deacon uttered, or the femur bone the woman in the next pew was kissing. Instead, it was the meal the faithful ate. This mystical meal answered to various names: Mass, Divine Liturgy, Eucharist, Lord's Supper, Love Feast, Holy Communion, and Table of the Lord.

When baptized Christians partook of the Lord's Supper, they were participating in a ritual that was just as spiritual as it was physical. Writing in the first decade of the 100s, Bishop Ignatius of Antioch believed that the Eucharist was "the medicine of immortality, the antidote against death and life forever through Jesus Christ."[29] In another letter written during the same time period, he emphasized that "the Eucharist is the flesh of our Savior Jesus Christ."[30] Justin Martyr, writing half a century later, agreed: "we do not receive these things as common bread nor common drink; but...we have been taught that the food eucharistized through the word of prayer...is the flesh and blood of that Jesus who became incarnate."[31]

> Writing about the mystery of the Lord's Supper, Cyril of Jerusalem asked in the fourth century: if, "by his own will, [Christ] once changed water into wine at Cana in Galilee...why should we not believe that he can change wine into blood?"[39]

Far from being a speck of bread and a shot of wine gulped down to memorialize Christ's death, the Eucharist was a direct encounter with God in the flesh. It was like coming face-to-face with Christ and uniting with him in body and soul. It was also a communal experience. Long before lone-ranger believers could home-order individual communion cups on the internet for individual consumption, early Christians were partaking of a common meal shared alike by all believers—living and dead. By ingesting the flesh and imbibing the blood of Christ, the believer was mystically linked with every other believer connected to Christ—whether those feasting on his body *on earth* or those abiding *in heaven*. As Jesus himself answered in response to the Sadducees, "He is not the God of the dead, but of the living" (Matt. 22:32; Mark 12:27; Luke 20:38).

HANGING UPSIDE DOWN IN MIDAIR

This is one of those sayings of Jesus's that sting our post-Enlightenment mindsets. In Christ, even when dead and without a living body, everybody is always alive. The ancients understood this much better than we moderns do. As Augustine wrote, "the souls of the pious dead are not separated from the Church." On the contrary, he added, "the faithful [dead] are still members of this [living] body, even when they have departed this life...That is why we read [in Revelation]... 'Blessed are the dead who die in the Lord.'"[32] According to the ancients, "dead" saints were as capable of hearing the prayers of the living and acting upon such prayers as if they had never died. At one of the most famous shrines among ancient Christians, the tomb of Saint Martin of Tours read: "Here lies Martin the bishop, of holy memory, whose soul is in the hand of God; *but he is fully here, present and made plain in miracles of every kind*."[33] This was no figure of speech. Early Christians believed that dead saints, though their souls were mystically in God's presence in heaven, were still present on earth, and they were aching to whisper their devotees' prayers into God's ears in heaven.

Modern Protestant Christians cringe at the notion that dead saints are out there actively answering prayers, healing sicknesses, comforting the afflicted, and exorcising the demons of the possessed. But this was nothing strange to the ancients. Their imaginative threshold was much higher than ours. They lived in an age of faith. They lived in an age of the miraculous. They lived in an age of wonder. Cataloging another day at the office, the Christian writer Jerome spoke of several dead saints in the Holy Land in the early 400s:

> [There were] many marvelous happenings. [There was] the noise of demons roaring in various torments, and, before the tombs of the saints... men howling like wolves, barking like dogs, roaring like lions, hissing like snakes, bellowing like bulls; some twisted their heads to touch the earth by arching their bodies backwards; women hung upside-down in mid-air, yet their skirts did not fall down over their heads.[34]

Demonic possession was a regular occurrence within ancient society, and the tombs and shrines of dead saints were like kryptonite to those possessed. Jerome's description, a pre-modern script for popular shows like *The Living Dead*, would not have astonished the ancients. As one historian explains, "Several accounts of martyr shrines [like this one] depict similarly chaotic and frightening scenes."[35]

KEEPING DEATH AT A DISTANCE

Just like there was never any golden age of the church when everyone got along, everyone tithed, and everyone knew the words to the Nicene Creed, there was never a golden age of church worship. Some early practices would not only turn heads today, such as the practice of a living person being baptized in behalf of a deceased family member,[36] others, such as the digging up of corpses at a public cemetery and wheeling their bloodied bones to church, would likely require time in jail or at least an appointment with a board-certified psychiatrist. Still, there were some common patterns in early Christian worship. There's no doubt that early Christians assigned mystery where we seek rational explanation, reveled in rituals where we seek pragmatism, and sensed a close connection with the deceased where we segregate ourselves from the dead and the dying. Put in terms we can understand: While our sin in the modern world may be keeping death as far away as humanly possible, in the ancient world it was losing no sleep after shooing away an unbaptized believer from the Communion table.

ENDNOTES

1 Ambrose, "Epistula 77," in *Ambrose of Milan: Political Letters and Speeches* (Liverpool: Liverpool University Press, 2005), 204.

2 Augustine, *City of God* 22.8, trans. Henry Bettenson (London: Penguin, 1984), 1034.

3 Ambrose, "Epistula 77," in *Ambrose of Milan*, 205.

4 Andrew McGowan, *Ancient Christian Worship: Early Church Practices in Social, Historical, and Theological Perspective*, Grand Rapids: Baker, 2014), 1.

5 Cyprian, "Letter 39," in *Saint Cyprian: Letters 1-81*, trans. Rose Bernard Donna (Washington, DC: The Catholic University of America Press, 1981), 100.

6 McGowan, *Ancient Christian Worship*, 245.

7 Quoted in Charles Freeman, *Holy Bones, Holy Dust: How Relics Shaped the History of Medieval Europe* (New Haven, CT: Yale University Press, 2011), 29.

8 Quoted in Peter Brown, *The Cult of the Saints: Its Rise and Function in Latin Christianity* (Chicago: University of Chicago Press, 1981), 7.

9 Freeman, *Holy Bones, Holy Dust*, 17.

10 Brown, *The Cult of the Saints*, 4 (italics added).

11 Robert Bartlett, *Why Can the Dead Do Such Great Things? Saints and Worshippers from the Martyrs to the Reformation* (Princeton, NT: Princeton University Press, 2013), 240.

12 Quoted in Michael Philip Penn, *Kissing Christians: Ritual and Community in the Late Ancient Church* (Philadelphia, PA: University of Pennsylvania Press, 2005), 79.

13 Penn, *Kissing Christians*, 2.

14 Tertullian, *On Prayer* 18, *The Ante-Nicene Fathers: Latin Christianity: Its Founder, Tertullian*, vol. 3 (Grand Rapids: Eerdmans, 1978; reprint), 686.

15 Tertullian, *To His Wife* 2.4, in *The Ante-Nicene Fathers*, vol. 4 (Grand Rapids: Eerdmans, 1956), 46.

16 Clement of Alexandria, *Paedagogus* 3.11, quoted in Penn, *Kissing Christians*, 1.

17 Athenagoras, *Plea for Christians* 32.5.

18 *Apostolic Tradition* 18.3.

19 *The Didache: The Teaching of the Twelve Apostles*, trans. Joseph Owles (CreateSpace Publishing, 2014), 16.

20 Tertullian, "On Baptism 4," quoted in McGowan, *Ancient Christian Worship*, 152.

21 Justin Martyr, "First Apology," in *The First and Second Apologies*, transl. Leslie William Barnard (Mahwah, NJ: Paulist Press, 1997), 66.

22 Novatian, "Treatise Concerning the Trinity," quoted in Christopher Hall, *Worshiping with the Church Fathers* (Downers Grove, IL: InterVarsity Press, 2009), 20.

23 Hippolytus, "The Apostolic Tradition," in *The Apostolic Tradition*, 45.

24 Cyril of Jerusalem, "Catechetical Lecture 20.2," in *Life and Practice in the Early Church: A Documentary Reader*, ed. Steven Alan McKinion (New York and London: New York University, 2001), 25–26.

25 So Peter Brown, *The Body and Society: Men, Women, and Sexual Renunciation in Early Christianity* (New York: Columbia University Press, 1988), 96.

26 David Hunter, *Marriage, Celibacy, and Heresy in Ancient Christianity: The Jovinianist Controversy* (Oxford: Oxford University Press, 2007), 46.

27 Quoted in Penn, *Kissing Christians*, 73.

28 Robin Jensen, *Understanding Early Christian Art* (Routledge: Oxford and New York, 2000), 175.

29 Ignatius, "Letter to the Ephesians 20.2," in *Ignatius of Antioch and Polycarp of Smyrna: A New Translation and Theological Commentary*, trans. Kenneth Howell (Zanesville, OH: CHResources, 2009), 90.

30 Ignatius, "Letter to the Smyrneans 7.1," in *Ignatius of Antioch and Polycarp of Smyrna*, 133.

31 Justin Martyr, "First Apology 66," in *The First and Second Apologies*, 70.

32 Augustine, *City of God* 20.9, trans. Henry Bettenson (London: Penguin, 1984), 916.

33 Quoted in Brown, *The Cult of the Saints*, 4 (emphasis added).

34 Jerome, *Letter* 103.13, quoted in Brown, *The Cult of the Saints*, 106.

35 Dayna Kalleres, *City of Demons: Violence, Ritual, and Christian Power in Late Antiquity* (Berkeley: University of California Press, 2015), 228.

36 See Paul's reference to this in 1 Cor. 15:29.

37 *Martyrdom of Polycarp* 18:2–3

38 St. Hilary of Poitiers, *The Fathers of the Church*, vol. 125, *Commentary on Matthew* (Washington, DC: The Catholic University Press of America, 2012), 53.

39 St. Cyril of Jerusalem, "Catechetical Lecture 22.2," in *The Christian Theological* Reader, ed. Alistair McGrath (Malden, MA: Wiley-Blackwell, 2011), 292.

Chapter 5

ARGUING WITH PAGANS AND JEWS—APOLOGETICS

It wasn't the finest example of Italian art. Michelangelo, Raphael, Leonardo da Vinci—these artists would have surpassed this crude stage of drawing when they were mere bambinos. But still, it's the earliest depiction of Jesus in the world. Hidden from sight for more than sixteen centuries, this crudely constructed piece of graffiti wasn't discovered until 1857. We don't know the artist's name, but we do know that he didn't think highly of Christianity—and that he had never taken an art class. The so-called Alexamenos Graffito depicts a young male slave worshiping a figure on a cross who bears the body of a man and the head of an ass. This ancient example of graffiti was drawn on a wall around the year 200 in the heart of Rome. The mockery of the primary figure, doubtfully a caricature of Jesus Christ, is heightened by its depiction from the rear. The crucified figure, explains classicist Michele George, is "dressed in a *colobium* (an item of servile clothing) without sleeves." This was the same type of clothing worn by the worshiping slave, meaning that the crucified man-ass and his adoring devotee were the lowest members of society.[1] In mangled Greek below the cross, this drawing can be derisively translated as "Alexamenos, worship (your) god."[2]

There have been several attempts to determine the exact context of this depiction, but here's a completely plausible interpretation—one that is strengthened by the discovery of a piece of graffiti translated from Latin as "Alexamenos, faithful" or "Alexamenos [is a] Christian" in close proximity. Historian of Rome Peter Keegan explains:

> a pagan sentry or doorkeeper in the imperial palace first sought to condemn a fellow guard by scratching on the wall, 'Alexamenos is a Christian'; when this did not result in the desired effect, he sketched a caricature of Alexamenos as the worshipper of a crucified god.[3]

Involving more than just lighthearted banter between two colleagues, Keegan postulates that a pagan doorkeeper repeatedly mocked a fellow guard (and likely slave) for being a Christian—perhaps under the conviction that anyone who believed in the deity of a crucified criminal was the intellectual equivalent of someone who today believes in Bigfoot. Whether or not this historical reconstruction—Bigfoot notwithstanding—completely captures the stories linking these shabby examples of graffiti, there's no doubt that early Roman society found Christianity utterly repugnant. Writing in 112, Pliny called Christianity "a depraved and excessive superstition"; three years later, Tacitus regarded it as a "pernicious superstition"; and in 122, Suetonius wrote that Christianity was "a new and mischievous superstition."[4] Either these highly regarded Roman intellectuals were working from the same religious playbook or they really disliked the rising sect of Jesus.

FIGHTING AN UPHILL BATTLE ON TWO FRONTS

If Christianity was going to survive, it didn't just need a public relations expert—it "needed defenders."[5] In its early days, the Christian religion was well poised to become the laughingstock of the ancient world. Unlike most every ancient religion, there were no animal sacrifices and no traditional priests. Neither were there any emperors or celebrities promoting it. On the contrary, the Christian religion was subversive, antisocial, and illegal—or at least not legally approved. Among a culture that highly valued tradition and was suspicious of novelty, Christianity lacked religious roots and was regarded as an irritating weed in need of uprooting. Worse still, its founder and object of adoration, a woodworker from a one-horse town, had three strikes against him: He was a laborer from the backwaters of Galilee, he was Jewish, and he was crucified as a criminal. Such things did not go unnoticed among the religious power brokers of the ancient world. Roman critics launched attacks and made disparaging comments against Christianity from the second century onward. In fact, the Romans were not the only ones who found Christianity lacking culture, intelligence, decency, and honor—the Jews were equally irritated. Whereas it took some time before Romans took notice of Christianity, it was not so easily camouflaged among Jews. To the contrary, the Jews knew where Christianity came from, and they were not impressed. A second-century Christian apologist summarized the situation facing the Christians best when he wrote, "By the Jews [we] are assaulted...and by the Greeks [we] are persecuted."[6] Wherever Christianity went, it had its critics well before its converts. It was fighting an uphill battle on two fronts.

"THE DREGS OF SOCIETY"

Roman rumors about early Christians are legendary. According to various critics, the Christians were atheists, seditionists, exclusivists, indigents, cannibals, dreamers, magicians, yokels, perverts, and prima donnas. Even the apostle Paul recognized the unimpressive stock of Christianity when he wrote to the Corinthians: "not many of you were wise by human standards; not many were influential; not many were of noble birth" (1 Cor. 1:26). But if we are looking for the most candid description of how Christians looked to the educated Roman world, we need not look any further than to second-century intellectual Marcus Cornelius Fronto who famously referred to Christians as the "dregs of society."[7]

It was Fronto, in fact, who leveled the charge against Christians that they worshiped the head of an ass, giving us context for the Alexamenos Graffito. Although he was not the first to make such an accusation, Fronto was horrified by the rumor that Christians worshiped a crucified man as well as the instrument of his torture: the cross. Not to be outdone by any man, however, whether he was considered the dregs of society or not, Tertullian, the feisty Christian who dished out just as much as he took in, mockingly responded to pagan Romans like Fronto: "You, in fact, worship the ass in its entirety, not just the head." Continuing on, he wrote in glittering rhetoric:

> And then you throw in Epona, the patron saint of donkeys and all the beasts of burden, cattle, and wild animals. You even worship their stables. Perhaps this is your charge against us that in the midst of all these indiscriminate animals lovers, we save our devotion for asses alone![8]

This type of exchange, though perhaps more comical than most, was rather common in the ancient world, and Christians responded in any number of ways to pagan critics.

"COPULATING IN RANDOM UNIONS"

When it came to worship services, Roman critics of Christianity were equally disdainful. Church services were widely exaggerated as involving the eating of human flesh, incest, and sexual orgies. Indeed, one of the most persistent rumors about Christianity was that its services encouraged and promoted desolate and riotous sex. Although it's tempting to brush aside such claims as clearly ridiculous and patently false, early Christians frequently responded to the accusation that their members were having sex during services. The counterattacks reach far back into the beginnings of the Christian movement, all the way back to the New Testament itself. As the book of Jude states, "certain intruders have stolen in among you…[who] defile the flesh." "These are blemishes," the author continues "on your love-feasts…they indulge in their own lusts" (Jude 4). Though the context is obscure, it's possible that aberrant leaders believing that the law of Christ gave them license to indulge in some serious free love during Christian "love-feasts." Second Peter acknowledges the same types of intruders who "indulge their flesh in depraved lust," who have "eyes of adultery," and are "insatiable for sin" (2 Peter 2:14).

As Christianity grew and became more public, sexual rumors intensified, though, to be sure, such actual sexual practices never represented the mainstream church. The Palestinian-born Christian philosopher Justin Martyr admitted that certain "Christians" were taking evangelistic efforts to the extreme, entertaining the rumor that certain aberrant services involved "upsetting the lamp [and] promiscuous intercourse."[9] According to third-century Christian apologist Minucius Felix, "upsetting the lamp" was a lurid sexual game played by deviant Christians when congregated:

> On a special day they gather for a feast with all their children, sisters, mothers—all sexes and all ages. There, flushed with the banquet after such feasting and drinking, they begin to burn with incestuous passions. They provoke a dog tied to the lampstand to leap and bound towards a scrap of food which they have tossed outside the reach of his chain. By this means the light is overturned and extinguished, and with it common knowledge of their actions; in the shameless dark with unspeakable lust they copulate in random unions.[10]

Despite the historical fog surrounding this practice, historian of antiquity Robert Louis Wilken believes that "there was some basis for such accusations."[11] Not only does Justin acknowledge that something strange was going on at *certain* Christian services (again, always in the minority), but so does his contemporary Clement of Alexandria. It was Clement who writes, for instance, that a particular group of Christians "overturn the lamps and so extinguish the light that the shame of their adulterous 'righteousness' is hidden, and they have intercourse where they will and with whom they will."[12] Expanding Paul's injunction to share a "kiss of peace" well beyond the letter of the law, such Christians turned church services into little more than community brothels.

Most scandalous of all, however, is the report of a religious service by a fourth-century bishop named Epiphanius. Whereas Clement of Alexandria was describing a heretical Christian group called the Carpocratians above, the following is an alleged account of a heretical Christian cult called the Phibionites. What you are about to read should come with a warning from the Surgeon General's Office, as it is highly disturbing and surely not good to one's health. Still, history is about the past, not about our preferences. Here is what Bishop Epiphanius of Salamis wrote about the Phibionites:

> After they have had intercourse in the passion of fornication they raise their own blasphemy to heaven. The woman and the man take the fluid of the emission of the man into their hands, they stand, turn toward heaven, their hands besmeared with the uncleanness, and pray...: 'We offer to [you] this gift, the body of Christ.' And then they eat it, their own ugliness, and say: 'This is the body of Christ and this is the Passover for the sake of which our bodies suffer and are forced to confess the suffering of Christ.' Similarly also with the woman when she happens to be in the flowing of the blood they gather the blood of menstruation of her uncleanness and eat it together and say: 'This is the blood of Christ.'"[13]

If such stories were true, it's easy to see why so many Greco-Roman pagans regarded Christianity with fear and trembling. The Roman Empire had its fair share of creepy "superstitions," but one that required the eating of semen and menstruating blood was in a league of its own. It makes little difference that those who may have practiced these rituals were Christian cults. As Lee Atwater once said, "perception is reality." The fact that some outsiders perceived of fringe Christians as practicing such peculiar rituals only confirmed for them that even mainstream Christians were doing so. For, unfortunately, detractors don't tend to cast their opponents in the best light.

'LET NO ONE SENSIBLE DRAW NEAR'

The second and third centuries of the Christian era have sometimes been regarded as the age of the apologists. These were scholarly figures who offered intellectual responses to the many criticisms leveled against Christianity at a time when the Christian faith was neither legally supported nor socially respectable. While some of the most prominent Christian apologists included figures such as Irenaeus, Clement of Alexandria, Justin Martyr, Tertullian, Origen, and Athenagoras, the three most prominent pagan apologists were Celsus, Porphyry, and Julian. Combined, these three pagan intellectuals attempted to shred Christianity to pieces. Their cases against Christianity were so strong, in fact, that later Christians destroyed their writings, forcing historians to cobble together their arguments from Christian apologists who quoted or alluded to their writings *while attempting to refute their claims*. Celsus, Porphyry, and Julian, a triple-threat to the faith, are a testament to early Christianity's shaky start. Like a baby colt new to the world, the church faltered for some time before its legs were strong. In hindsight, we know that Christianity prevailed in the ancient world, but back then there was every likelihood that Christianity would disappear like countless other mystery religions or cults. Like dying stars, such religions flickered for a moment before going completely dark in the cosmos of world history.

> The Greek word *apologia* referred to speech of defense in the law courts. Not surprisingly, those Christians who offered a defense of the faith against religious opponents came to be called *apologists*. Works written by apologists were naturally most common before the adoption of Christianity as an official religion.

Beginning with the earliest critic, Celsus was a Greek intellectual who wrote a stinging rebuke against Christianity called *True Doctrine* around the year 170. The Christian theologian Origen wrote a lengthy reply to Celsus about seventy years after the book was written and well after Celsus was dead. Unlike many others who had a distaste for Christianity but had never imbibed its teachings and writings, Celsus had actually read the Bible and studied Christian authors. He had done his homework, in other words, and was all too happy to share his research with the world. Recognizing that Christianity emerged out of Judaism, he thought Christians were full of contradictions: "Who is wrong?" he asked "Moses or Jesus?"[14] Both taught, he believed, completely different religions. According to Celsus, the Christians were a bunch of religious quacks whose founder was a magician from a barbarian land. He argued that "it was by magic that [Jesus] was able to do the miracles which he appeared to have done."[15] He also thought Jesus was a pot that called the kettle black. Though "a drunkard himself," he had the audacity of staggering into keg parties like an inebriated resident director accusing college students of being drunk.[16] In terms of the book ends of Jesus's life—his incarnation and passion—Celsus was not impressed. Reflecting on Jesus's incarnation, Celsus asked, "Is it only now after such a long age that God has remembered to judge the human race? Did He not care before?"[17] As for Jesus's death, Celsus found it shameful and pitiable: "[Jesus] was not helped by his Father, nor was he able to help himself."[18] If the former were true, God was a monster; if the latter were true, Jesus was powerless. Either way, it struck Celsus as ironic that Christians were supposed to only worship one God yet they believed that Jesus was to be praised alongside his Father.

Not surprising given his low regard for Jesus, Celsus was equally critical of Jesus's followers. To him, the Christians were nothing more than a band of "illiterate and bucolic yokels."[19] Amusing himself, since his humor does not seem to have caught on among the Christians, Celsus emended one of Jesus's saying to: "Let no one educated, no one wise, no one sensible draw near. For these abilities are thought by us to be evils. But as for anyone ignorant, anyone stupid, anyone uneducated…let him come boldly."[20] In short, Celsus thought the Christians a bunch of bottom feeders who avoided evangelizing people with a higher education and public standing in exchange for "only the foolish, dishonourable, and stupid, and only slaves, women, and little children."[21] The Christian religion was not only asinine and an affront to all decorum, it was only heralded by the riffraff of the Roman Empire.

> The overwhelming majority of Christians at this time could neither read nor write. But we shouldn't think that they were still unaware of major disputes taking place. Ancient writers occasionally remarked how ordinary people were just as involved in theological disputes as the intellectuals who wrote about them.

'THE FIERCEST ENEMY OF THE CHRISTIANS'

Celsus was by no means the only major critic of Christianity. In many ways, Porphyry and Julian were much more influential in the anti-Christian tradition of the pagan world. Porphyry, who flourished in the late third century, was heralded by Augustine of Hippo as "the most learned of the philosophers" and "the fiercest enemy of the Christians."[22] So piercing were his criticisms that many of the brightest Christians thinkers of their day responded to him over the course of several generations: Eusebius, Methodius, Arnobius, Lactantius, Apollinarius, Jerome, and Augustine. Porphyry apparently wrote a book called *Against the Christians* that took full aim at the Bible and another called *Philosophy from Oracles* that was directed at Jesus's disciples and the theology of the Christian sect. Unfortunately, for his sake, Porphyry was too smart for his own good; and it's very difficult to piece together his arguments since all his writings were destroyed.

'AGAINST THE GALILEANS'

So, too, were the writings of Julian, who lived in the following century during a time when Christians could no longer be described as "the dregs of society." Julian's *Against the Galileans* was one of the last great treatises against Christianity in the ancient world. It attacked Christianity from the inside out, striking blows at the Bible, Jesus and the disciples, Christian theology, and common church practices. Baptized and educated as a Christian as well as a relative of Emperor Constantine, Julian turned the full force of the law against the Christian religion when he became emperor in 361. He not only barred Chris-

Sarcophagus of Julian on Left in Istanbul, Turkey.
Courtesy of G.dallorto.

tians from being educators, but he closed down churches to consecrate them as pagan temples. Out of pure scorn, he also attempted to restore the Jewish temple in Jerusalem and repopulate the Holy City with Jews. All of these actions earned Julian the epithet "the apostate." Julian, however, would not have regarded himself as an apostate, but a restorer. In Julian's estimation, it was the Christians who were the real apostates. It was they who had abandoned the customs of their fathers (Jewish or Roman) in exchange for "that new-fangled Galilaean god."[23] It was they who had rejected animal sacrifices. And it was they who had shirked away from their civic responsibilities as citizens of the empire.

At a time when the study of civics is at an all-time low in the United States, it's hard for many of us to understand how important civic duty was to traditionalists like Julian. To the Greeks and Romans, there was no such thing as private religion or lone-ranger citizenship. To exist was to be part of a community. It's what it meant to be human. As Aristotle famously wrote, "man is a political animal."[24] As a political animal, every person was expected to play his or her part for the good of society. Each person's actions, good or bad, affected the community as a whole. The Romans were of one accord with the Greeks when it came to one's civic duties. In the eyes of Romans such as Julian, the Christians rejected *Romanitas*—what we may call the essence of what it meant to be Roman. Christians engaged in societal sabotage—the undermining of *Romanitas*—by turning their backs on the Roman gods, by refusing their civic duties, and by disregarding the customs and beliefs of their forefathers. This was the original sin of Christianity, and it was unforgivable. By creating an alternate society with a different God, customs, and morals, the Christians abandoned and effectively invoked a curse on the very foundations of Roman civilization. Julian keenly understood this. He did everything humanly possible to destroy his boyhood (Christian) faith since it, he was fully convinced, was doing everything it could to destroy the empire.

> After only eighteen months on the job, Julian was struck down in battle by an opponent. Christians conjectured that it was a dead saint who rightly dealt him the death blow for rejecting the Christian faith. Regardless of exactly how Julian died, it was no secret how he lived: He was a living sacrifice on the altar of paganism, and with more time he could have seriously threatened Christianity.

According to Wilken, the most effective weapon Julian used against Christianity was its fractured relationship with Judaism. This has always been "the Achilles' heel of the Christian tradition."[25] In Julian's estimation, the Christians were guilty of apostasy for rejecting Jewish monotheism and Jewish interpretation of the Hebrew Bible. Julian exposed this concept with such insight that one of his Christian adversaries, writing in the next century, confessed that "None of our teachers is capable of rebutting or refuting his works."[26] Because Julian knew the Scriptures as well as any other educated Christian, he used Old Testament prophetic passages to disarm the New Testament. Well aware of the Christological interpretation of Deuteronomy—that "I will raise up for them a prophet like you from among their fellow Israelites" (18:18) as referring to the coming of Jesus Christ—Julian stressed that this passage said nothing about the person whom God would raise up being divine. On the contrary, Julian taunted, the "prophet will be like [Moses—and therefore human] and not like God."[27]

THE ORIGINS OF CHRISTIAN ANTI-SEMITISM

But it wasn't just the Romans who criticized early Christianity. It was also the Jews. The name of authors who responded to Jewish criticism by writing tracts against Judaism is a Who's Who List of Early Christian Celebrities. Justin, Tertullian, Origen, Cyprian, Eusebius, Ambrose, Jerome, Augustine, Gregory of Nyssa—these were the most prominent teachers of the early church, and they each leveled attacks against Christianity's mother religion. Like the perennial debate between whether the chicken or the egg came first, it's tough to say whether animosity between Judaism and Christianity was first hatched among Christians or Jews.

According to many scholars, one of the reasons early Christians began attacking Judaism was because the Jewish faith was actually thriving at a time when Christianity was merely surviving. In his classic study of early Christianity and Judaism, Marcel Simon wrote that "the most compelling reason for Christian anti-semitism was the religious vitality of the Jews."[28] It's easy to think that Judaism simply walked off the platform of religious history after Jesus took center stage and only returned for a cameo in the twentieth century, but that's not what happened. Truth is, Judaism was a serious religious competitor to Christianity for several centuries—perhaps even longer. Despite two costly wars against Rome in the first and second centuries, and the absolute destruction of the city of Jerusalem, Judaism adapted to its new settings and found a way to not only survive but thrive. Judaism, though ridiculed among the Greeks and Romans, was still recognized as a religion with roots; but the same could not be said about that wild branch that sprouted from the base of the tree.

'YOU STUPIDLY STUBBORN PEOPLE'

Justin Martyr, though by no means the first Christian apologist against Judaism, was one of the most influential. He was an intellectually curious philosopher who had flirted with many ancient superstitions before tying the knot with the Christian movement. While residing in Ephesus in the 130s, he reportedly met and debated a Jewish man named Trypho. During this time, cities like Ephesus, Alexandria, and Antioch were teeming with Jewish communities. Like old lovers who awkwardly pass each other on the street corner but look the other way, Christians and Jews would have regularly seen each other in their daily lives. For his part, Justin welcomed debate with Trypho, pouncing on his new Jewish friend with gusto.

Assessing his arsenal of intellectual weapons, Justin flung them one by one at Trypho; when required, he also engaged in defense. In his explanation for why Christians no longer observed the Law of Moses, Justin lunged forth with strong rhetoric. "The law [of Moses]," he explained, "is already obsolete, and was intended for you Jews only, whereas the law of which I speak is simply for all."[29] While Trypho was not looking, Justin also managed to sneak the Hebrew Bible out of his, and his fellow Jews', possession. In his frustration, Justin noted that Trypho did not understand the prophecies of Christ "contained in your Scriptures, or rather not yours, *but ours*."[30] Justin lashed out at the Jews' refusal to see Christ everywhere predicted and prophesied in the Hebrew Bible: "you…stupidly stubborn people…are neither wise nor understanding, but sly and treacherous."[31] One gets

***Justin Martyr* by André Thévet.**

Ancient Ephesus. Courtesy of Ad Meskens.

Justin Martyr was a highly influential apologist living in the second century. Originally from Palestine, he immigrated to Rome in the middle of the second century, where he was an active teacher. As his name suggests, he was martyred for his faith—sometime around the year 165.

the impression from reading Justin that Jesus was lurking around every bush and tree in the Old Testament with a nametag and a megaphone. The only reason why the Jews did not notice him was because they obstinately read the Bible with eyes averted, ears clogged, and heart closed. At the end of their debate, Trypho registered his appreciation, wished Justin a safe voyage to Rome, and no doubt rocked himself to sleep that night. Fluent in Christianese, Justin parted company with Trypho with one last exhortation: "[may] you come to believe entirely as we do that Jesus is the Christ of God."[32]

'THIS IS WHY I HATE THE JEWS'

Justin's longwinded debate with Trypho served as a template for Christian defenses against Judaism. For centuries, Christian theologians composed tracts against Judaism like they were writing dissertations for graduate degrees. You weren't anybody in the church unless you could defend yourself against the religion of the Jews. Regardless of whether we chalk up all this anxiety about Judaism to paranoia, loathing, insecurity, or righteous indignation, the Jews were the whipping boys of early Christian rhetoric like the Anabaptists would be during the Protestant Reformation. One of the most blatant rhetorical attacks against Judaism came from a preacher living in Roman Antioch. In the year 386, well before pastors today began preaching sermon series like "Eight Ways to a Better You," John Chrysostom was going from one cantankerous sermon series to another. Although his nickname *Chrysostom* is Greek for "Golden-mouth," his mouth more often resembled a potty than gold when it came to the topics of Judaism, heresy, and women. Interrupting his tirade against Arian Christians to launch a preaching campaign against Jews and Christians sympathetic to Jewish rituals, John Golden-mouth took Christian anti-Semitism to new levels of racist rhetoric. We might well label his sermon series "Eight Reasons I Hate Judaism." It was that hateful.

"The aim of [John's] sermons was to dissuade Christian Judaizers from participating in Jewish rites and to demonstrate the truth of the Christian religion...In the mind of the early Christians there was no middle ground between Judaism and Christianity. Only one could be right."[40]

Golden-mouth's first homily in *Against the Jews* set the tone for the rest of the sermons. For him, the race of Abraham was better known as "miserable Jews." Although they "had been called to the adoption of sons, they fell to kinship with dogs." They were like beasts "unfit for work… [but] fit for killing…fit for slaughter." Their place of worship, the synagogue, was "a dwelling of demons…a place of idolatry." Their condition in life was "not better than that of pigs or goats." They abhorred God and were guilty of "plundering…covetousness…abandonment of the poor… thefts…[and] cheating in trade." Their worship was an "abomination." Worst yet, John thundered forth, "they committed the crime of crimes… the slaying of Christ,"[33] a common charge that reverberated throughout the Middle Ages.

The rest of John Golden-mouth's sermons were equally venomous. This powerful preacher was livid that some of his parishioners were visiting Jewish services during special festivals of the year. He didn't care that they were curious about the people with whom God had covenanted since time immemorial—he wanted them to flee the synagogue of Satan before their very souls were demonically possessed. Fully convinced that the Lord was on his side, he channeled the anger and judgment of God to the Judaizing Christians in his congregation. Turning a deaf ear to Jesus's words "Father, forgive them for they know not what they do" (Luke 23:34), Chrysostom bellowed forth in his sixth homily: "You [Jews] did slay Christ, you did lift violent hands against the Master, you did spill his precious blood. This is why you have no chance for atonement, excuse, or defense." It was while preaching this spiteful sermon that John revealed why he self-professedly "hated" the synagogue and the Jews. "This is my strongest reason for hating the synagogue: it does have the Law and the prophets. And now I hate it more than if it had none of these…This is why I hate the Jews. Although they possess the Law, they put it to outrageous use."[34]

***Relief of John Chrysostom.* Courtesy of Jastrow.**

Although we recoil today at Golden-mouth's rhetoric, he was convinced, as he later stated, that the "martyrs would [have been] glad to hear this discourse."[35] He considered himself the holy mouthpiece of God, and was doing nothing more than following the clear commands of Scripture and the models of the apostle Paul, who dealt the Jews "a knockout blow and said enough to shut their shameless mouths"[36] when citing Scripture against them. Truth be told, John Golden-mouth was a beloved pastor, a caretaker of the poor, and a highly adored speaker. He was, in fact, the greatest Christian orator of his day, who had to be secretly removed from Antioch when he was chosen as bishop of the imperial capital so as not to incite a riot among his adoring congregation. He was so revered that his golden rhetoric glittered for centuries, exercising "an enormous influence on later Christian attitudes toward the Jews."[37] In the year 388, for instance, Bishop Ambrose of Milan condoned the burning of a synagogue; and Cyril of Alexandria expelled all the Jews in his city, where they had lived in peace for centuries, shortly after he became bishop in the year 412.[38] These actions, sad to say, were just the birth pains of the violence that Christians would deliver in the Middle Ages. In a strange twist of fate, the very heroes of the Christian faith who did so much good in this world were also the haters of outsiders like the Jews. Sinful saints like John Golden-mouth and Ambrose of Milan spoke out of both sides of their mouths when offering the words of eternal life.

SILENCING THE OPPOSITION

If early Christianity needed its defenders to survive, what did other religions need when Christianity ascended to dominance? In the year 313, Constantine made Christianity a legally recognized religion, and in 380 Theodosius made Christianity the official religion of the Roman Empire. And then, in the 390s, Theodosius completely forbade pagan sacrifice. It is a testimony of the sheer religious monopoly of Christianity that it eradicated its opposition. Disregarding Jesus's parable for the wheat and the tares to exist side-by-side until harvest time, ancient Christians became impatient reapers. Growing accustomed to power, Christianity increasingly had little patience for social gadflies and intellectual critics. The three most cogent and compelling tracts written against the Christian religion were all systematically destroyed. The books by Celsus, Porphyry, and Julian were too dangerous to leave in the hands of readers, even though most of the population couldn't read, so they were burned to ashes. Perhaps early Christians were afraid that such criticisms would negatively impact the faithful or perhaps they thought they were an insult to the integrity of God. Whatever the case, we only know about these influential writings because Christians quoted portions of these when preparing their counterattacks.

Although it took a while for Christianity to find its voice against critics, it did not take it long to use that voice as a weapon. It's easy to sympathize with Christian apologies in the early years because Christians were the underdogs of the ancient world. But after becoming the alpha dog, some Christians bit into their opponents with ferocity. As historian Ralph Novak explains, "violence became more endemic as bishops directed bands of monks, soldiers, and urban Christian mobs against pagans [and] Jews."[39] After the Roman Empire institutionalized as a Christian society, legislation was enacted against Christian dissidents, threatening the very existence of paganism and Judaism. The sect that was originally labeled a "depraved and excessive superstition" was fast becoming something much more potent than ever envisioned by Romans or Jews. Although it did not shake from itself all of its depraved and excessive remnants, it grew into a religion of unbridled power. It was, in fact, becoming a force to be reckoned with.

ENDNOTES

1 Michele George, *Roman Slavery and Roman Material Culture* (Toronto: University of Toronto Press, 2013), 28.

2 George, *Roman Slavery and Material Culture*, 29.

3 Peter Keegan, *Graffiti in Antiquity* (Oxford: Routledge, 2014), 108.

4 Quoted in John Dominic Crossan, *The Birth of Christianity: Discovering What Happened in the Years Immediately after the Execution of Jesus* (New York: HarperOne, 1998), 3. The writings come from *Letters* 10.96, *Annals* 15:44.3, and *Nero* 16.2, respectively.

5 Robert Louis Wilken, *The Spirit of Early Christian Thought: Seeking the Face of God* (New Haven, CT: Yale University Press, 2003), 4.

6 "The Epistle of Diognetus 5.17," in *The Apostolic Fathers*, ed. Michael Holmes (Grand Rapids, MI: Baker, 1998; 2nd ed.), 299.

7 Quoted David White, *Tertullian the African: An Anthropological Reading of Tertullian's Context and Identities* (Berlin: Walter de Gruyter, 2007), 114.

8 Tertullian, "To the Nations 9," in Quincy Howe, *Tertullian of Africa: The Rhetoric of a New Age* (Bloomington, IN: iUniverse, 2011), 84.

9 Justin Martyr, "First Apology 26," in *The Fathers of the Church*, vol. 6, *A New Translation*, trans. Thomas Falls Washington, DC: The Catholic University Press of America, 1977), 63.

10 Marcus Minucius Felix, Octavius 9," in *The Octavius of Marcus Minucius Felix*, no. 39 (New York: Paulist Press, 1974), 65. See Robert Louis Wilken, *The Christians as the Romans Saw Them*, 2nd ed. (New Haven, CT: Yale University Press, 2004), 18–19.

11 Robert Louis Wilken, *The Christians as the Romans Saw Them* (New Haven, CT: Yale University Press, 2003; 2nd ed.), 19.

12 Clement of Alexandria, *Strometeis* 3.2.10.

13 Epiphanius of Salamis, *Panarion* 26.4-5, quoted in Wilken, *The Christians as the Romans Saw Them*, 20.

14 Origen, *Contra Celsum* 7.8, trans. Henry Chadwick (Cambridge: Cambridge University Press, 1980).

15 Origen, *Contra Celsum* 1.6, 10.

16 Origen, *Contra Celsum*, 3.76, 179.

17 Origen, *Contra Celsum*, 4.6, 188.

18 Origen, *Contra Celsum*, 1.55, 50.

19 Origen, *Contra Celsum*, 3.54, 164.

20 Origen, *Contra Celsum*, 3.44, 158.

21 Origen, *Contra Celsum*, 3.49, 162.

22 Quoted in Wilken, *The Christians as the Romans Saw Them*, 127, 151.

23 Ibid., 177.

24 Aristotle, *Politics* 1.253.

25 Wilken, *The Christians as the Romans Saw Them*, 195.

26 Ibid., 197.

27 Ibid., 190–91.

28 Marcel Simons, *Verus Israel: A Study of the Relations between Christians and Jews in the Roman Empire (135-425)*, trans. H. McKeating (Oxford: Oxford University Press, 1986), 232.

29 Martyr, "Dialogue with Trypho 11," in *The Fathers of the Church*, 164.

30 Martyr, "Dialogue with Trypho 29," in *The Fathers of the Church*, 191 (emphasis added).

31 Martyr, "Dialogue with Trypho 123," in *The Fathers of the Church*, 339.

32 Martyr, "Dialogue with Trypho 142," in *The Fathers of the Church*, 366.

33 John Chrysostom, "Against the Jews 1.1.5, 1.2.1, 1.2.6, 1.3.1, 1.4.1, 1.7.1, 1.7.2 in *The Fathers of the Church*, vol. 68, *A New Translation*, trans. Paul Harkins (Washington, DC: The Catholic University of America, 1979), 3, 5, 8, 11, 14, 25, 26.

34 Chrysostom, "Against the Jews 6.2.10, , 6.5.9, 6.5.11," in *Saint John Chrysostom*, 155 and 171.

35 Chrysostom, "Against the Jews 6.1.7," in *The Fathers of the Church*, 149.

36 Chrysostom, "Against the Jews 7.4.2," in *The Fathers of the Church*, 190.

37 Robert Louis Wilken, *John Chrysostom and the Jews: Rhetoric and Reality in Late Fourth Century* (Eugene, OR: Wipf & Stock, 2004), xv.

38 John Gager, *Origins of Anti-Semitism: Attitudes toward Judaism in Pagan and Christian Antiquity* (Oxford: Oxford University Press, 1983), 120.

39 Ralph Novak, *Christianity and the Roman Empire: Background Texts* (Harrisburg, PA: Trinity Press International, 2001), 167.

40 Robert Louis Wilken, *The First Thousand Years: A Global History of Christianity* (New Haven, CT: Yale University Press, 2012), 109.

Chapter 6

DRAWING A FAMILY TREE—THEOLOGY AND ECCLESIOLOGY

Like a zoologist carefully analyzing a genetically mutated species, the Italian bishop was dissecting one theological abnormality after another. His tome on Christian heresy, written during the late fourth century, was nearing completion—even if no one was ever going to read it. According to *Butler's Lives of the Saints*, this ole clergyman had earned a reputation "as a seeker-out of heretics."[1] This was a favorite pastime of early bishops enjoying the rising prestige of the church after the conversion of Emperor Constantine. During the course of his research and writing, the Italian bishop had come a long way since classifying a Gnostic sect called the Ophites as the début heresy in human history.[2] Now, almost 160 heresies later, he could confidently relinquish his pen under the knowledge that he had dealt a death blow to Christian heresy.

The Temptation and Fall of Eve* by William Blake found in Milton's *Paradise Lost.

Or maybe not. Contrary to common wisdom, knowledge is not always power, even when backed by the church. Bishop Philastrius's *Book on Christian Heresy* was not only ignored by most of his peers but it was also completely incapable of curbing popular enthusiasm for lousy theology. Dispassionately dissected or not, Christian heresy was not going away. It, like a cancer in a body, was here to stay. Philastrius was simply one of many ancient leaders involved in the church's tag-and-release program. Justin Martyr, writing in the middle of the second century, tagged several individuals and movements as heretical but was powerless to shield them from unsuspecting Christians. Writing to the Roman emperor in a book titled *First Apology*, Justin alluded to a "treatise [composed] against all the heresies that have existed."[3] Whenever this treatise was written, it would have been out of date the moment the ink dried. Christian heresy, far from disappearing as the church swelled in numbers and power, was destined to expand from an inkblot to a puddle and beyond.

CHRISTIANITY'S FIRST BLACKLISTS

As we have discussed in detail, the early church never experienced a golden age of unity, peace, and hand-holding holiness. On the contrary, theological brawls, nasty splits, and highhanded name-calling has marked Christianity since the beginning. To be sure, there have also been moments of harmony and seasons of concord, but there's no use trying to cover up the repeated schisms of the church. Far from living into the reality of being "the [singular] body of Christ" (1 Cor. 12:27) as the apostle Paul so eloquently described in the New Testament, the church is more fittingly depicted as "the multiple bodies of Christ"—broken in bits because we can't get along well. Many groups have been unwilling and ill-disposed to recognize most others as legitimate members of the church. Rather than working through our differences, we Christians have a recurring habit of picking up our ball, exchanging words, and leaving the playground when others play by slightly different rules. Living in a world today that contains nearly 50,000 different Protestant denominations, it doesn't seem that we've learned much from our past. We Christians are part of a tradition that has grown accustomed to thinking in black-and-white categories and in the realm of us-versus-them. We have grown accustomed to dogmatically distinguishing orthodox insiders from unorthodox outsiders.

As the early church began to take shape, it didn't take long for believers to launch a whole category of books against the unorthodox of the Christian tradition—against those who pretended to be followers of Christ but who were really disciples of the Devil. These so-called "heresy catalogues" contained the original blacklists of Christianity. They designated in no-nonsense language all and sundry who deviated from the narrow path of the truth. As historian Geoffrey Smith explains, "the composition, circulation, and consultation of heresy catalogues became important means by which ecclesiastical leaders could protect their communities from the threat of false teachers and their teachings."[4] Since false teaching went hand in glove with the emergence of the church, heresy catalogues were the stuff of second-, third-, and fourth-century Christianity. Some of the most prominent heresy catalogues appeared in Hippolytus's *Refutation of All the Heresies*, (Pseudo) Tertullian's *Against All Heresies*, Philastrius's *Book on Christian Heresy*, and Epiphanius's *Medicine Chest*. But they could also appear in the writings of orthodox authors such as Clement, Irenaeus, Origen, Jerome, and Augustine.

Wherever they appeared, these heresy catalogues were aflame with indignation. With eternal salvation at stake, orthodox Christian writers

According to Rowan Greer, "'heresy' normally refers to a false religious sect or to erroneous teaching and is consequently the opposite of 'orthodoxy.' Heresy therefore remains…a denial of orthodox doctrine."[32]

pointed their swords at folks like Simon Magus, Basilides, Valentinus, Marcion, Montanus, and Arius as harbingers of hell. Writing in the second century, the heresy catalogue appearing in the writings of Hegesippus bemoaned such "false Christs, false prophets, false apostles who split the unity of the Church by poisonous suggestions against God and against His Christ."[5] These frauds had to be named and denounced, and there was a whole army of Christian authors willing to sign up for the task. As they were deployed, very specific theological parameters were created in order to identify the true followers of Christ from false ones.

Table 6.1. Notorious Blacklisted Christians in the Early Church

Names (and Dates)	Region	Views Deemed Heretical
Simon Magus (1st century)	Samaria (in Israel)	Made himself out to be a God; there was reportedly a statue made of him and worshiped
Marcion (2nd century)	Pontus (in northern Turkey)	Concluded that the God of the Old Testament was different from that of the New Testament; anti-Jewish and suspicious of the body and of matter; constructed his own biblical canon, containing ten of Paul's letters and a highly edited version of Acts
Basilides and Valentinus (2nd century)	Alexandria (in northern Egypt) and Rome	Both taught Gnosticism, namely, that the body was bad while the soul was good and that Christianity was passed on through secret knowledge rather than through common rituals
Paul of Samosata (3rd century)	Antioch (in southwest Turkey)	Believed that Jesus was born a man but later adopted by God the Father as the Logos or Word of God
Arius (2th century)	Alexandria (in northern Egypt)	Held that God is one and indivisible, that the Son is a creature of God, and that the Son and the Spirit are subordinate to God the Father
Apollinaris (4th century)	Latakia (in western Syria)	Argued that Jesus had a human body but that he didn't have a human mind (only a divine one)

Death of Simon Magus. Courtesy of Kramden.

BEFORE THERE WAS ANCESTRY.COM

According to early heresy catalogues, Simon the Magician was the first false prophet to poison the church's well. In lurid language, he was variously described by orthodox heresy-hunters—called *heresiarchs* by scholars today—as the architect of deceit, the heretic of hell, and the first-born of Satan. The English word *simony*, which means to purchase one's religious office rather than earning it through character or competence, was coined with Simon's image in mind. Though his description in the book of Acts was hardly flattering, church fathers speculated that Simon the Magician showed a predilection toward pushing his own ungodly agenda and lusting after power. Unwilling to play second fiddle to the apostles, Simon composed his own tune and began recruiting backups—lots of them.

It didn't take long for church fathers to make the connection between Simon the Magician and that other Simon who featured so prominently in the New Testament: Simon the Fisherman. Like black and white, hot and cold, right and wrong, it was only reasonable to infer that Simon the Magician would have a spiritual counterpart to balance the evil of the universe. The fact that these two counterparts shared the same name was simply icing on the cake. Writing in the late second century, Bishop Irenaeus of Lyons began tracing the heritage of all orthodox Christianity to the good Simon, the rock on which Christ had determined to build his church, while simultaneously drawing the ancestry of all heretical Christianity to the bad Simon, the sand on which Satan had decided to build his wicked empire. Just as Simon Peter formed a link to the truth of Christ's teachings, so Simon Magus became "the founder of a chain of deviant teachings."[6] It was a stunningly simple argument, but it had profound consequences.

> For early Christians, pedigree was of profound importance. No one was anyone unless he or she could trace lineage to someone of (prior) significance. By drawing a family tree of truth and untruth, orthodoxy and heresy, Christians would forever know who belonged to the family of heaven and who belonged to the family of hell. Just like the Old Testament priesthood of the Levites passed from father to son in an unbroken line of succession, so the priesthood of Jesus passed from apostles to bishops.

The official doctrine that Irenaeus developed to distinguish the family of true Christians from that of false ones has been called *apostolic succession*. According to historian Robert Williams, "Succession was a well-known concept in institutional history in the Hellenistic world. It established, 'after the fact,' that certain officials, those in a succession, were rightful possessors of authority in an institution."[7] Fully aware of how countless Christian sects claimed to be the sole heirs of Christ's teaching, church fathers were desperate to discover a way to distinguish right from wrong and the true church from the false one. The doctrine of apostolic succession filled that void.

In his multi-volume *Against Heresies*, Irenaeus made a clear distinction between the "tradition which originates from the apostles, which is preserved by means of the succession of presbyters in the Churches," and the tradition of the bad Simon, which had produced "many offshoots of numerous heresies."[8] Knowing that Simon the Magician's tradition had regrettably been "scattered throughout the whole world,"[9] there were simply too many heretical branches—and too many orthodox ones, for that matter—to list name by name. So Irenaeus proposed a much simpler means by which to judge between heretical and orthodox branches: Allow the heritage of the church in Rome to decide it all. As he explained, "it is a matter of necessity that every Church should agree with this [Roman] Church, on account of its preeminent authority." Because "the apostolical tradition ha[d] been preserved continuously" in the Roman church, he continued, it was necessary to check one's orthodoxy in comparison to it.[10] The boxing ring had been prepared and the people were getting ready to rumble: It was Simon the First Bishop of Rome versus Simon the First Magician of the World.

> Irenaeus laid out the following succession of leadership in Rome in *Against Heresies* 3.3.3: Jesus → Peter (and Paul) → Linus → Clement → Evaristus → Alexander → Sixtus → Telephorus → Hyginus→ Pius → Anicetus → Soter → Eleutherius. There had been twelve generations of leadership after Jesus, and each of these bishops was believed to have preserved the truth of the gospel without adding anything.

WINNER TAKES ALL

Irenaeus's plan to allow the heritage of the church in Rome to clench the greatest theological controversy in the second century had profound ramifications on the history of Christianity, not least of which was to prop up the legacy of the bishop of Rome—that is, the pope—as the default adjudicator of Christian doctrine and practice. Unlike the pope, who could demonstrate an unbroken succession of leadership through Peter to Jesus himself, leaders not able to establish "primitive succession" to one of the apostles were to be "held in suspicion." Such men were "heretics of perverse minds" and "schismatics puffed up" with pride.[11] Rather than tracing their ancestry to Christ and his apostles, they were successors of the arch-schismatic Simon the Magician.

Although Irenaeus's logic may not sway many modern-day Christians, there was a method to his madness. Living in an age when the

Scriptures were regarded by many early Christians as "ambiguous, and that the truth [could not] be extracted from them,"[12] Irenaeus took three truths for granted when it came to Christian authority. First, the apostles would have transmitted the essentials of the faith to those they entrusted as leaders, namely, bishops; neither apostles nor their successors would have added or removed anything from the gospel record. Second, the successors to the apostles would have imparted that same teaching to their successors—generation after generation after generation. Finally, any supposed Christian leader who taught something out of step with what the bishops who could trace their line of succession to the apostles taught was, by definition, a heretic, for it was not possible for secret knowledge to have eluded the ancestors of Christ. Case closed. The first round goes to Simon the First Bishop of Rome.

MEASURING FAITH

Tertullian, a Christian writer living a generation after Irenaeus, agreed. He had cut his teeth on theological argumentation, and he was more than willing to describe those he disagreed with as sandbags of Satan. Much like Martin Luther more than a millennium later, Tertullian was cranky, shrewd, outspoken, sarcastic, and highly influential—all wrapped up in one overbearing yet pious persona. An educated rhetorician living in Roman North Africa, Tertullian wrote more than thirty works before his death in the middle of the third century. His *Prescription against the Heretics* was an early Christian classic, and his aggressive yet articulate opposition to heresy set a model for centuries to come.

Like Irenaeus, Tertullian taught that church authority derived "from the Lord's apostles."[13] Christianity was not about individual convictions or theological innovation. It was not about lone-ranger leaders letting their imaginations run as wild as stallions with new beliefs or private cogitations. It was about preserving the deposit of truth that had been handed down to the bishops of the church by the apostles themselves, and it was about faithfully delivering that truth to the world. It was that simple. In glittering rhetoric, our spirited friend Tertullian yelled, "Away with all attempts to produce a mottled Christianity...With our faith, we

> Tertullian's *Prescription against the Heretics* used a technical term in the title that would have been immediately understood by his readers but goes over our heads today. *Praescriptio* in Latin was a Roman term meaning to dismiss a legal case before it comes to trial on account of a technicality. By using this legal term here, Tertullian was indicating that heretics didn't have any right to discuss Christianity. Their claim to be able to argue with orthodox Christians was invalid.

desire no further belief."[14] All that was necessary for Tertullian was simple trust in the tradition—affirmation of what he called "the rule of faith," that is, the basic teaching of Christianity as later codified in the Apostles' and Nicene Creed.[15] "To know nothing in opposition to the rule (of faith)"—that was "to know all things."[16] That was how Tertullian understood the truth.

Table 6.2. The Apostles' Creed and the "Rule of Faith"

For the most part, the "rule of faith" to which Tertullian referred was summarized in the Apostles' Creed, a second-century document originating in Rome. This creed—along with the Nicene Creed, which is very similar—is the most concise doctrinal statement of Christianity. Organized into four parts (God the Father, God the Son, God the Spirit, and the Church), it is read as follows:

"I believe in God, the Father Almighty, creator of heaven and earth.

I believe in Jesus Christ, his only Son, our Lord. He was conceived by the power of the Holy Spirit and born of the Virgin Mary. He suffered under Pontius Pilate, was crucified, died, and was buried. He descended to the dead. On the third day he rose again. He ascended into heaven, and is seated at the right hand of the Father. He will come again to judge the living and the dead.

I believe in the Holy Spirit, the holy catholic Church, the communion of the saints, the forgiveness of sins, the resurrection of the body, and the life everlasting."[17]

According to Tertullian, the only legitimate "offspring of apostolic churches" were those descendants who taught nothing more and nothing less than the apostles themselves taught.[18] When it came to "the rule of faith," the burden of proof was on those who claimed to have received a different tradition from what the twelve apostles themselves taught and practiced. In evocative language, Tertullian unrolled his argument before the heretics:

> But if there be any (heresies) which are bold enough to plant themselves in the midst of the apostolic age, that they may thereby seem to have been handed down by the apostles, because they existed in the time of the apostles, we can say: Let them produce the original records of their churches; let them unfold the roll of their bishops, running down in due succession from the beginning.[19]

Demanding the equivalent today of a DNA test to determine whether a child and a father are genetically related, Tertullian challenged his opponents to a simple test: Let's see if the doctor can link your DNA with that of the apostles. That is to say, let's see if your family tree matches that of the successors to Christ. If Tertullian's opponents could prove their apostolic ancestry, he would accept their churches as legitimate bodies of Christ. But if they couldn't, they were to be rejected as bastards of the faith—what he called the "disinherited."[20] For if such weren't rightful descendants to the apostles, Tertullian explained, "they cannot be true Christians."[21]

ARRESTING BAD THEOLOGY

Despite the advantage of apostolic succession and the rule of faith when it came to deciding between right and wrong doctrine and practice, rival claimants to Christianity did nothing but mushroom from the second century onward. It's true that certain questionable "churches" could be held in suspicion since they couldn't establish their first-century origins, but even bishops with a respectable lineage, one scholar notes, "could disagree as to what followed the apostolic faith, and what was orthodox in one church could be regarded as heretical in another."[22] While any red-blooded Protestant would cheerfully surrender this dispute to the Scriptures themselves to adjudicate, early Christians understood that the Bible was often the source of the greatest interpretative confusion. Heretics routinely appealed to the Scriptures for their peculiar viewpoints. Truth is, bemoaned an early Christian monk named Vincent of Lérins, "a distinguishing mark of heretics is that they always have a thousand [biblical] citations at hand." As much as we would like for Scripture to interpret itself by convincing heretics of their nefarious ways, this monk—more than a thousand years before the Protestant Reformation made this painfully obvious—acknowledged that "Scripture seems to have as many interpretations as there are interpreters."[23] As we have discussed about the toy Lite-Brite, we get a completely different design depending on which template of interpretation we use. It wasn't that heretics were necessarily abandoning the Bible—they were simply appealing to different verses.

> Many scholars call those early believers who eventually came to be regarded as the Catholic and Orthodox Churches as the "proto-orthodox." They do this as a way to distinguish them from the many other groups of Christianity that disappeared or were condemned by the proto-orthodox as heretics.

With so much on the line, and with the Bible itself often serving as the source of conflicting interpretations, it was necessary for a third party "to adjudicate charges of heresy" among rival groups.[24] This opportunity came in the early fourth century. There was one crucial development that had made such an international body of Christian gatekeepers not only possible but capable of arresting bad theology: the newfound power of majority Christians, thanks to the conversion of Emperor Constantine to Christianity, to enforce their decisions not only by lawful decree but by brute force. The so-called Great Church was emerging (what we now call the Catholic Church and Eastern Orthodox Church), and it would be a powerful force to be reckoned with for those diverging from their view of orthodoxy.

FROM *CHRISTIANITAS* TO *COSA NOSTRA*

Love him or hate him, Emperor Constantine was the godfather of the Christian *familia*. Under the constraints of the Roman cultural practice of patronage, Constantine's adoption of Christianity made him the legal guardian of the Christian faithful: the *pater familias*. With some exaggeration, *Christianitas* or "Christianity" for Constantine and his advisors was now *Cosa Nostra*—"Our Thing." In a strange twist of fate given its humble heritage, the Christian household was now Constantine's family to run as he saw fit. Although his concern for good Christian theology was potentially less spiritual and more pragmatic in nature—after all, the *pax ecclesia* contributed to the *Pax Romana*—he developed a keen interest in the first worldwide dispute of the early church: the so-called Arian controversy at the Council of Nicea. And, according to our records, he even proposed the term that ended the first phase of the controversy: *homoousios* ("of the same substance" in Greek).

Statute of Constantine **from Capitoline Museum in Rome by I, Jean-Christophe Benoist.**

GOD TALK

For quite some time—all the way back to the first century, in fact—Christians had argued amongst themselves over the nature of God. The most acute arguments revolved around the identity of Christ. Was Christ

God? If so, in what way? Was Christ begotten before time or was he made in time? Did Christ have a human body or merely a divine outer shell? Was the human Jesus adopted by God to be his Messiah while on earth, while in heaven, or not at all? Now, in the early fourth century, these seemingly ivory-tour disputes were coming to a head at a time when the mechanisms for dealing with them were not proving effective. The Christological dispute at hand involved a spirited priest of Alexandria named Arius and his disheartened bishop named Alexander. What was the nature of the dispute? In a word, Father Arius was teaching that Christ was the highest creation of God, but that Christ wasn't equal to God in divinity since God was indivisibly one. In his own words, Arius apparently believed that this was "the faith and thought of the Church and of the holy scriptures."[25] Whether he was right or wrong, Arius's fate—indeed, his eternal salvation—was now in the hands of others. It was now in the hands of the emperor.

The dispute that arose from Arius's teaching became the primary item of agenda for the first ever worldwide (or "ecumenical") church council. After assembling together bishops from all across the Roman Empire (though precious few came from the West), Constantine at last entered the hushed hall of the assembly at Nicea bedecked in his customary purple and gold rob. After taking the seat of honor at the center of the gathering, he delivered a short speech in Latin, which was immediately translated into Greek since few of the bishops understand that language. According to our gushingly partial yet still primary source for the proceedings—Eusebius of Caesarea's *Life of Constantine*—the emperor, though not even baptized and thus not legally regarded as a "real" Christian, was actively involved in the deliberations of the council, "until at last he succeeded in bringing [the bishops] to one mind and judgment respecting every disputed question,"[26] particularly as it related to theological matters regarding the nature of the Godhead.

Arius at the Feet of the Emperor Constantine at Council of Nicea. Courtesy of Jjensen.

Probably at the suggestion of the emperor's ecclesial advisor (who happened to be the facilitator of the council), Constantine suggested to the bishops that the word *homoousios* (in Latin, *consubstantialis*) best characterized Jesus Christ's relationship to God the Father, meaning that the Father and the Son shared the same stuff of divinity. That is, if the Father was God and the Son was God's Son, then the Son must also be God. Constantine's term was not agreeable to all bishops for a variety of reasons. Even Peter Leithart, in his tightly argued *Defending Constantine*, conceded that "the pleas for peace [from the emperor] had the effect of shutting down debate and silencing the most effective speakers."[27] Constantine, whether an unbaptized non-bishop or not, was still the leader of the ancient world, and his language eventually won the day. Whether this was accomplished by sheer intimidation, politicking prudence, or divine providence, we may never know. Out of the two hundred or three hundred bishops attending the council, only two lifelong friends of Father Arius objected to the extra-biblical and philosophically laden term *homoousios*. Many other bishops bit their tongues in disgust, but still put their John Hancock's on the creed.

For many such bishops, their initial reluctance to sign the creed probably had less to do with the actual word *homoousios* and more to do with the unbridled denunciation of Arius's theology appended to the creed. In wording that would make any lawgiver blush with envy, the legal case against Arius was, for all practical purposes, closed:

> And those that say 'There was when he was not,' and 'Before he was begotten he was not,' and that 'He came into being from what-is-not,' or those that allege that the son of God is 'of another substance or essence,' or 'created,' or 'changeable,' or 'alterable,' these the Catholic and Apostolic Church anathematizes.[28]

In no uncertain language, the soul of the spirited priest Arius was thrust outside the community of faith like a man with leprosy. Rumor has it, in fact, that Saint Nicholas, the man who would become Santa Claus, gave Arius the gift of a broken jaw. Saint Nick punched Arius right in the face. Arius's theology, indeed, his whole person, was *anathema*—cursed, disavowed, excommunicated. Although this was a harsh penalty, the leaders of the faith believed that the essence of Arius's teaching was spiritual poison that threatened a person's very life. Better the death of one dissident cleric than that of a thousand impressionable churchgoers.

EIGHTY CONCUBINES BUT ONLY ONE BRIDE

The creed formulated by the Council of Nicea was one of the most definitive statements ever recorded in church history. It was one of the earliest sketches of the ancestry of the church and became a simple way to distinguish true Christians from false ones. Unfortunately, despite its best intentions, it did not completely eradicate false branches of Christianity from growing out of the root. Writing a few decades after the death of Constantine, Bishop Epiphanius of Salamis was fully aware that heresy had not simply continued after Constantine's heroic defense of the truth at Nicea but that it had multiplied. While being outdone by his colleague Bishop Philastrius in terms of the sheer number of heresies he catalogued, Epiphanius exchanged quantity for quantity. In his book against heresy, charmingly entitled *Medicine Chest* but more recently labeled "the quintessential example of Christian heresiology in late antiquity,"[29] Epiphanius drew succor from the spiritual salve of the Song of Songs. "There are sixty queens and eighty concubines," the theologically love-struck bishop wrote, but "My dove, my perfect one, is the only one." Translated into common parlance: While there were eighty concubines that figuratively bore Christ's name but despised it in their faith, so there was only one legitimate and undefiled wife. This one bride, Mother Church, alone contained the truth, while the scores of concubines—"Christian" heretical bodies—languished in error. It was Epiphanius's intention, he explained in the introduction to his work, to provide a "chest of remedies for those whom savage beasts have bitten."[30]

> Arguments between the Nicene party of Christians and Arians was more than theological trash talk. It was also a game of economics. Athanasius of Alexandria was accused by Arian Christians of depriving them of their ration of grain but of ensuring that it made its way to those aligned with his theology.

According to proto-orthodox believers, savage beasts had been ravishing the body of Christ since Pentecost. In fact, the heresy catalogues that developed in the second century found their basis in the New Testament itself, which was layered thick with responses to heretical teachings of the faith. The Christian religion was destined to become a battlefield for right belief and practice—ultimately gaining a victory for orthodoxy, now backed by the state, in opposition to its opponent, heresy. As the late first-century document *The Didache* so clearly stated, "There are two ways, one of life and one of death, and there is a great difference between these two."[31] Though variously described, the way of life was that of the twelve apostles, that of the biblically faithful, and that of the true believers. This was the way toward life since it led directly to Jesus Christ, the source of life itself. The other way, by contrast, led directly to hell. Not necessarily paved in good intentions, it was the way of the chief apostates, of the biblically faithless, and of the false believers. These faithless freethinkers, far from being legitimate children of Christ, were regarded by faithful sons and daughters as theological bastards. There was one family of Christ. All others were impostors. Well before ancestry-based websites recognized that they could make millions by helping a country of immigrants discover their family's buried roots, ancient Christians understood that one's lineage to a man from Nazareth was more precious than gold itself.

ENDNOTES

1 Alban Butler, *Butler's Lives of the Saints*, New Full Edition (Collegeville, MN: Liturgical Press, 2000), 143.

2 Philastrius, *Liber de Haeresibus*, Patrologia Latina 12:1113–114.

3 Justin Martyr, *First Apology*, 26.

4 Geoffrey Smith, *Guilt by Association: Heresy Catalogues in Early Christianity* (Oxford and New York: Oxford University Press, 2015), 48.

5 As quoted by Eusebius, *The History of the Church* 4.22, trans. G. A. Williamson (London: Penguin, 1989), 129.

6 Pheme Perkins, "Schism and Heresy: Identity, Cracks, and Canyons in Early Christianity," in *The Routledge Companion to Early Christian Thought*, ed. D. Jeffrey Bingham (Oxford and New York: Routledge, 2010), 229.

7 Robert Williams, *Bishops Lists: Formation of Apostolic Succession in Ecclesiastical Crises* (Piscataway, NJ: Gorgias Press, 2005), 229.

8 Irenaeus, "Against Heresies 2.2.2 and 1.28.1," in *The Ante-Nicene Fathers: The Apostolic Fathers with Justin Martyr and Irenaeus*, ed. Alexander Roberts and James Donaldson, vol. 1 (Grand Rapids: Eerdmans, 1975), 415, 353.

9 Irenaeus, "Against Heresies 1.10.2," 331.

10 Irenaeus, "Against Heresies 3.3.2," 415.

11 Irenaeus, "Against Heresies 4.26.2," 497.

12 Irenaeus, "Against Heresies 2.2.1," 415.

13 Tertullian, "Prescription 6," 246.

14 Tertullian, "Prescription 7," 246.

15 Tertullian, "Prescription 13," 249.

16 Tertullian, "Prescription 14," 250.

17 *The Apostles Creed: A Faith to Live By*, ed. C. E. B. Cranfield (London: Continuum, 2003), 3.

18 Tertullian, "Prescription 20," 252.

19 Tertullian, *On the Prescription of Heresies* 32.1.

20 Tertullian, "Prescription 37," 261.

21 Tertullian, "Prescription 37," 261.

22 Rowan Greer, "Heresy," in *Encyclopedia of Early Christianity*, 2nd, ed., ed. Everett Ferguson (New York and Oxford: Routledge, 1999), 520.

23 Vincent of Lérins, "Commonitorium," in Thomas Guarino, *Vincent of Lérins and the Development of Christian Doctrine* (Grand Rapids, MI: Baker, 2013), 5.

24 Greer, "Heresy," in *Encyclopedia of Early Christianity*, 520.

25 Quoted in A. H. M. Jones, *Constantine and the Conversion of Europe* (Toronto: University of Toronto Press, 1978), 147.

26 Eusebius, Life of Constantine 3.13.

27 Peter Leithart, *Defending Constantine: The Twilight of an Empire and the Dawn of Christendom* (Downers Grove, IL: InterVarsity Press, 2010), 169.

28 "The Creed of Nicea," in Henry Bettenson, ed. *Documents of the Christian Church*, 2nd ed. (London, Oxford, and New York: Oxford University Press, 1967), 25.

29 Todd Berzon, “Known Knowns and Known Unknowns: Epiphanius of Salamis and the Limits of Heresiology,” *Harvard Theological Review* 109, no. 1 (2016): 76.

30 *The Panarion of Epiphanius of Salamis*, Book 1, ed. Frank Williams (2009), 3.

31 “The Didache 1:1” in *The Apostolic Fathers*, ed. Michael Holmes, 2nd ed. (Grand Rapids, MI: Baker Academic, 1989), 149.

32 Rowan Greer, “Heresy,” in *Encyclopedia of Early Christianity*, 2nd, ed., ed. Everett Ferguson (New York and Oxford: Routledge, 1999), 520.

Chapter 7

READING IN THE FORBIDDEN SECTION—THE OTHER CHRISTIAN BIBLE

He was making rounds within his diocese when he startled upon the strange document. Recently appointed bishop of the cosmopolitan city of Antioch in the late second century, Serapion was the eighth bishop of the city where Jesus-followers were christened as *Christians* and he was the sixth bishop after the famous bishop Ignatius. As bishop of a large city, Serapion was frequently required to visit smaller parishes within his diocese in order to offer guidance, guarantee religious conformity, and make sure everyone knew that he was in charge. This time, around the year 200, he was in the tiny village of Rhossus in what is now a small coastal town in the southern region of Turkey, less than a hundred miles from Antioch. While visiting with the Christians there in the backwaters of the Roman Empire, Bishop Serapion encountered a charming idiosyncrasy. Rather than reading communally from one of the more esteemed biographies of Christ's life, such as the Gospel of Matthew or the Gospel of John, the Christians in Rhossus were reading some peculiar book called the *Gospel of Peter*. Assuming that anything named after Jesus's right-hand man must be theologically above board, the old bishop smiled in approval and went his way.

Returning to Antioch, however, the illustrious city in which the Gospel of Mat-

Greek Manuscript of *Gospel of Peter*. Courtesy of Henry Barcley Swete (1835–1917).

thew was probably written and where the apostle Peter had served as its first bishop, Serapion had come to his senses. The charm of village life had petered out. "When I visited you," the distressed bishop wrote back to the provincials in Rhossus, "I assumed that you all clung to the true Faith; so without going through the 'gospel' alleged by them to be Peter's, I said, 'If this is the only thing that apparently puts childish notions into your heads, read it by all means.'" But after securing a copy of the *Gospel of Peter* for himself and reading through this book allegedly written by the chief apostle of Christ, Bishop Serapion looked like he had seen a ghost. Far from reinforcing what Serapion and his fellow bishops had received about the story of the Savior, the *Gospel of Peter* made faint suggestions that Jesus was not fully a man and that he did not suffer on the cross. In haste, the bishop prepared a pamphlet called *The So-Called Gospel of Peter*, which enumerated line by line where this wayward, would-be gospel had gone astray. After receiving this pamphlet attached to the bishop's letter, the Christians at Rhossus very likely burned the *Gospel of Peter* to ashes, as Serapion made it clear that he was going to "make every effort to visit you again; so expect me in the near future."[1] Now at last, Bishop Serapion could rest at ease knowing that he had diverted his flock in Rhossus from the pits of hell, and that the spurious *Gospel of Peter* had been laid to rest.

'DAMNED IN THE INEXTRICABLE SHACKLES OF ANATHEMA FOREVER'

But that wouldn't always be the case. In 1887, as Bishop Serapion's bones were no doubt turning over in his grave, French archaeologists working in Egypt discovered the tomb of an ancient Christian monk clasping the dreaded *Gospel of Peter* as if for dear life. For centuries this dastardly document had lay buried under the earth, invisible to vigilant bishops and unable to pervert the minds of their gullible flocks. But now, in the dawn of the modern world, the dead document had been resurrected, stirring others to ponder what other naughty pseudo-Christian treasures lay buried beneath the sands of time. Perhaps there were other "gospels" that ancient Christians had squelched in secrecy, which would one day come to light as skeletons in early Christianity's closet.

> One of the most fascinating discoveries of secretive Christian documents occurred in Nag Hammadi, Egypt in 1945. Almost fifty different texts were discovered such as the *Gospel of Thomas* and the *Secret Book of James*.

When all is said and done, the coming to light of titillating texts from the ancient past, including the discovery of the Gospel of Peter in 1887, has convinced many good folks that the public has been duped. Why didn't all the "lost scriptures" written by early Christians make it into the biblical canon? Are these older than the New Testament documents? Was Dan Brown's *The Da Vinci Code* right after all? These are certainly fair questions, though we might want to reconsider our strategy if our primary source of ancient history comes from a modern murder mystery such as Brown's book. Unfortunately, as is so often the case, history has been overshadowed by histrionics. Truth is, early church leaders were fully aware of "secret scriptures" or "hidden gospels." This was nothing new to them.

Indeed, early church leaders like Serapion were quite familiar with such scriptures, whether the *Gospel of Judas* or the *Gospel of Thomas*. But they were hardly impressed. Whether we interpret their reactions to them as paranoia, prejudice, or just good policy, they regularly berated believers who aided and abetted the writing or reading of these illicit documents. Writing in the middle of the fifth century with fiery prose, Pope Leo I denounced any bishop who did not burn apocryphal writings to dust:

> It is…necessary…that the false books…shall not be used in any practice of reading. The apocryphal writings—under the name of the apostles [but really] a breeding ground of many falsehoods—must not only be forbidden, but also entirely removed and burnt by fire. Although…these writings…have an appearance of piety, they are…never without venom...Therefore a bishop who does not prohibit the apocrypha from being owned in the houses or who permits these books…to be read in church under the name of canonical writings…knows that he will be condemned as a heretic.[2]

***Pope Leo I* by Francisco Herrera the Younger.**

Leo wasn't the only one aghast at the false books competing with the true books of Scripture. In his tome on early heresy written in the late fourth century, Bishop Philastrius scolded the various Christian groups that made use of the "secret scriptures, that is, the apocrypha."[3] (Here he is referring to the so-called New Testament Apocrypha, not the Old Testament Apocrypha, which were Jewish texts included in the most ancient

Old Testaments and written hundreds of years *before* Christ.) According to most Christians, there were only twenty-seven legitimate New Testament books, and any additional ones were seedbeds of sin. Countless popes, the self-styled heads of the Christian Church, agreed. In the early fifth century, Pope Innocent I censured "other books" mistakenly believed to be on par with Holy Scripture, stating in grave and somber language that "they are not only to be rejected but also condemned."[4] Similarly, in the sixth century, the so-called Gelasian Decree, based on the reported sayings of Pope Gelasius, outlawed the use of dozens of illicit scriptures. So severe was this papal prohibition of the authors and adherents of such apocryphal literature that they were "to be damned in the inextricable shackles of anathema for ever."[5]

Figure 7.1. Select Examples of New Testament Apocrypha

Literary Type	Titles	Possible Dates by Century
Gospels	*Gospel of the Egyptians* *Gospel of Mary* *Gospel of Peter* *Gospel of Thomas*	2nd 2nd 2nd 2nd
Acts	*Acts of John* *Acts of Paul and Thecla* *Acts of Peter* *Acts of Thomas*	2nd 2nd 2nd 3rd
Epistles	*Epistle of Barnabas* *Third Epistle to the Corinthians* *Epistle to the Laodiceans* *Epistles of Paul and Seneca*	2nd 2nd 2nd 4th
Apocalypses	*Apocalypse of Paul* *Apocalypse of Peter* *Second Discourse of the Great Seth* *Secret Book of John*	4th 2nd 3rd 2nd

NAUGHTY OR JUST CURIOUS?

Eternal shackles or not, there was only one problem with the "repetitive repudiation of apocryphal writings"[6] among early church authorities. The more attention drawn to the secret scriptures of the Bible, the more bishops and leaders incited the curiosities of their prying parishioners—leading us to believe that ancient Christians were just as naughty as modern ones. Despite frequent and fervent prohibitions, and the throwing around of some eternally damning decrees, early Christian leaders were virtually powerless at curbing popular enthusiasm for the "forbidden" books of the Bible. According to historian Els Rose, evidence from medieval lectionaries makes it "abundantly clear" that these scriptures were regularly read (= heard) and enjoyed by Christian believers.[7] Living in an age before cable television, cars, and YouTube, it's hardly surprising that Christians turned to sensational scriptures as sources of amusement and speculation.

What did these secret scriptures say, and why did people write them? There's every indication to believe that many apocryphal books were simply the products of curious Christians who wanted to fill in the juicy details of their heroes' lives. Although the Christian Apocrypha unsheathed its imagination on various biblical and non-biblical figures, it's only natural that Jesus became the apple of the Apocrypha's eye. After all, inquiring minds wanted to know more about their Savior, and the New Testament was not willing to cooperate. Not only do we get from the Gospels a mysteriously meager ration of Jesus's forty days on earth after he did the unimaginable—enter death and walk away unscathed—but we have an abbreviated picture of his two or three years of ministry. Even the Gospel of John acknowledges that "there were many other things that Jesus did" (21:25) that neither he nor the other canonical authors discussed. And we can forget about details from Jesus's childhood, adolescence, and career. It's just not there.

> The New Testament reports on less than ten percent of Jesus's actual life. That's right—less than ten percent! Other than a very brief account of Jesus's birth (and one story from Luke about the time he was twelve), the Gospels only cover select moments of the last two or three years of Jesus's life of about thirty-three years.

Figure 7.2. Criteria for Books Included in the New Testament

Though not an exact science, there are several reasons why a book *eventually* was included in the New Testament canon:

- Apostolicity: It was linked with an apostle.
- Antiquity: It was not recently written.
- Usage: It was widely read and accepted.
- Orthodoxy: It taught established teachings and practices.

Books that could not prove apostolicity, antiquity, widespread usage, and orthodoxy became non-canonical or extracanonical. That didn't necessarily mean they were evil or heretical—on the contrary, there were several books like *First Clement* and the *Didache* that were widely commended—they were just not the stuff of Holy Scripture.

Was Jesus smiley or serious, short or tall, bearded or clean shaven? Did he ever break a bone or catch the flu, argue with his friends, or get a measurement wrong for a cabinet he was making? How often did he pray, could he speak Greek or Latin, and did he have curative powers as a child or teenager? In short, what did Jesus do for three whole decades before putting away his carpenter's toolbox and putting on the cloak of messiahship? The four canonical Gospels don't say, and we can hardly blame curious Christians for wanting to know more than the less than ten percent of Jesus's life that the New Testament actually discusses.

JESUS AS A CHILD: THE INFANCY GOSPELS

The so-called Infancy Gospels are some of the more entertaining books of the New Testament Apocrypha. Here is where our suspicions are confirmed that Jesus must have dazzled his boyhood friends with magic like the ancient equivalent of David Blaine, and that he must have also been involved in some good-hearted mischief like he was Ashton Kutcher. Here also is where our suspicions are confirmed that Jesus's mother, Mary, must have been as sanctified as her son. It's in one of the earliest Infancy Gospels, the second-century *Protogospel of James*, where we learn of Mary's perpetual virginity—before (*ante partem*), during (*in partu*), and after giving birth (*post partum*). As is still commonly affirmed among Eastern Orthodox Christians, this gospel narrates that Joseph was an elderly widower who married the young and sexually continent Mary as the winner of an ancient lottery. The two never had sexual intercourse, and all of Jesus's brothers and sisters were from Joseph's first marriage. So central was Mary's virginity in this book that even after giving birth miracu-

Young Jesus Raising Clay Birds to Life.
Based on Infancy Gospel of Thomas.
Courtesy of Beat Estermann.

lously to Jesus at the tender age of sixteen, a skeptical friend of the midwife named Salome entered the birth cave in Bethlehem and actually "inserted her finger [inside Mary] to test her condition." For "tempting the living God" by such a lack of faith, if not borderline blasphemy, Salome's hand was "consumed by fire."[8] It was only after an angel commanded her to place her scorched hand on the Baby Jesus that Salome was instantly healed.

Scholars debate whether Infancy Gospels were fanciful stories divorced from reality or based on kernels of historical truth. These texts appear to have become popular beginning in the second century, meaning that they probably say more about the communities that wrote them than the Jesus they wrote about. Examples of Infancy Gospels include the *Infancy Gospel of Thomas*, the *Protogospel (= Protoevangelium) of James*, the *Gospel of Pseudo-Matthew*, and the *Gospel of the Infancy*.

Whereas the *Protogospel of James* narrates the birth of Jesus, the second-century *Infancy Gospel of Thomas* speculates about what life was like for Jesus (and his unwary neighbors) between the ages of five and twelve. Contrary to what we might expect from the sinless Savior of the world, Baby Jesus was a very naughty boy. He was disobedient and volatile. At the age of five, when other kids were playing with wooden dolls, Baby Jesus was making twelve sparrows out of clay on the Sabbath in violation of Old Testament commandments. After his father reproved him for doing work on the Sabbath, Jesus brought the sparrows to life and commissioned them to fly away. On another occasion, after a child disturbed his playing area, Jesus zapped the kid senseless, yelling out "You unrighteous, impious ignoramus… Behold, you shall…wither as a tree."[9] And he did.

Young Jesus Accused of Pushing a Boy off a Roof. **Based on Infancy Gospel of Thomas. Courtesy of Beat Estermann.**

According to this non-canonical infancy gospel, Jesus earned a back-street reputation for obliterating other children, and he was eventually accused of tossing one of his hapless peers off a housetop roof. In a plea for innocence, Jesus shouted to the dead boy on the street, "'rise up and tell me, did I throw you down [or not]?' [The dazed boy] immediately rose up and said: 'No, Lord, you did not throw me down, but you raised me up.'"[10] Although Jesus matured during his tween years, he still had a violent streak. After one of his teachers hit him on the head for being a smart aleck, Jesus cursed the teacher and telepathically forced him to the ground. Despite moments of malice, however, Jesus the Tween was occasionally willing to help those in need. He healed his brother James of a deadly snake bite and also brought back other youths from death. The *Infancy Gospel of Thomas* ends with Jesus's trip to Jerusalem during Passover at the age of twelve, the seed of which story comes from Luke's Gospel.

FROM INFANCY TO SECRECY: GNOSTIC CHRISTIANITY

Despite intriguing stories about Jesus's life as an infant and tween in the so-called Infancy Gospels, it was the secret details about Jesus's life as an adult that have become the bailiwick of apocryphal Christianity. These adult accounts of Jesus's life do not necessarily speculate about his "hidden years," but they oftentimes present a completely different picture of who Jesus was and what he came on earth to accomplish. The term for many of these apocryphal texts is Gnosticism. Who were these Gnostic Christians, and what did they believe? Hidden in the term *Gnostic* is the Greek word meaning "knowledge" (*gnosis*), and we can conclude that Gnostic Christians were the ones who were really "in the know"—or so they thought.

> "A wicked world; a wicked god who made it; salvation consisting of rescue from it; and rescue coming through the imparting of secret knowledge, especially knowledge that one has the divine spark within one's own self. Those are the four distinguishing marks of Gnosticism."[21]

Gnostic Christians claimed that a divine spark existed in every person from a heavenly realm, and that this spark needed to be (re-)ignited by secret revelation in order to understand our true selves and escape the wicked world in which we live. In Gnostic apocryphal writings, Jesus came to earth as a sort of "God-in-a-bod"—a divine being who only appeared to be a man with flesh—to reveal secret knowledge to those with ears to hear and eyes to see. Apparently, there weren't many such people. As we might expect from books claiming secret knowledge, Gnostic Christian texts are as perplexing as they are pleasurable to read; they more closely resemble

Buddhist sutras than Christian scriptures. Many of the documents discovered at Nag Hammadi in the mid-twentieth century in Egypt have been classified as Gnostic, and early mainstream Christians who encountered such Gnostic teaching and writings regularly condemned them for denigrating the flesh, muddying the simplicity of the gospel, rejecting the (God of the) Old Testament, and speculating—or just plain falsifying—the life and teachings of Christ.

JESUS THE BUDDHIST-CHRISTIAN SAGE: THE *GOSPEL OF THOMAS*

Did Jesus really have a twin brother? Well before Monty Python's *Life of Brian* broadcast on the big screen how horribly humorous life could have been like for a Jewish man born the same day Jesus was, there were several Gnostic scripts in the ancient world claiming that Jesus Christ had a twin brother. His name, familiar to most Christians today, was Thomas. But here's the kicker: *Thomas* was not a formal name but a nickname, and the nickname meant "twin." In Aramaic—the language Jesus, Thomas, and the other disciples spoke—the term *Thomas* described a twin brother, which is why this person was often called *Didymus* as well—the Greek term for "twin." Syrian Christians believed that Judah, one of the four brothers of Jesus listed in the Gospels of Matthew and Mark, was Jesus's twin brother—usually called Judas Thomas or Didymus Judas Thomas. The *Gospel of Thomas* claims to be written by Jesus's twin brother, and the *Acts of Thomas*, another second-century Christian apocrypha, shows Jesus and his twin brother Thomas ministering side-by-side in India, where they were preaching the good news of celibacy, of all things! (See more about that story in Chapter 9 of this book.)

We see many of these characteristics in one of the most controversial Gnostic texts, the *Gospel of Thomas*. In this second-century text discovered fully intact at Nag Hammadi, Jesus is showcased as a sort of Buddhist-Christian sage who confounds his readers with enigmatic expressions and cryptic conversations. Its opening line discloses "the hidden sayings that the living Jesus spoke and Judas Thomas the Twin recorded."[11] The remaining one-hundred and fourteen sayings in this Gnostic gospel reveal a very un-Jesus-like Jesus. There are no stories about Jesus's birth, baptism, travels, miracles, death, or resurrection. Instead, there is Jesus the Galilean guru, a philosopher who would have given the Dalai Lama a run for his money. When asked by the disciples if they would enter the kingdom of heaven as babies, the Gnostic Jesus replied:

> When you make the two into one, and when you make the inner like the outer and the outer like the inner, and the upper like the lower, and when you make male and female into a single one, so that the male will not be male nor the female be female, when you make eyes in place of an eye, a hand in place of a hand, a foot in place of a foot, an image in place of an image, then you will enter [the kingdom]. (Saying 22)

While these types of sayings give most of us headaches, they were salve to Gnostic Christians.

Continuing on in the document to Saying 70, Jesus said to his disciples, "If you bring forth what is within you, what you have will save you. If you do not have that within you, what you do not have within you [will] kill you." The *Gospel of Thomas* concludes with Saying 114, which has been one of the most intriguing of our Galilean guru's teaching:

> Simon Peter said to [the disciples], 'Mary [Magdalene] should leave us, for females are not worthy of life.' Jesus said, 'Look, I shall guide her to make her male, so that she too may become a living spirit resembling you males. For every female who makes herself male will enter heaven's kingdom.'

As baffling as this saying is to modern readers, it was the stuff of Gnostic Christianity. Jesus didn't come to save sinners; he came to save spiritual "males" who disparaged the things of this world.

JESUS'S GIRLFRIEND: MARY MAGDALENE IN THE *DIALOGUE OF THE SAVIOR* AND THE *GOSPEL OF PHILIP*

But Jesus also came to save females, even though he might have to turn them into males first. The final saying in the *Gospel of Thomas* piques our interest in the relationship between Jesus and Mary Magdalene. Does Saying 114 suggest that the disciples were angry with Mary Magdalene because she was monopolizing their Galilean guru's attention? Does it imply that the two were more than friends? Though taken from other sources, Dan Brown's *The Da Vinci Code* popularized the belief that Jesus and Mary Magdalene were secret lovers—a rumor of at least eighteen hundred years.

Fortunately for those seeking sensational claims about the ancient past, there are interesting sources for their

> The second-century *Pistis Sophia* showcases the wisdom of Mary Magdalene and pushes the male disciples of Jesus to the margins. Despite Peter's complaint to Jesus that "we cannot endure this woman who gets in our way and...talks all the time," Jesus praises Mary for her advanced wisdom, saying "Well done, Mary, pure spiritual woman."[22]

***The Penitent Magdalene* by Domenico Tintoretto.**

speculation. Although the New Testament documents are relatively muted when it comes to describing Mary Magdalene's role in the life of Jesus, several apocryphal texts arouse our curiosity. The oldest dialogue between Jesus and Mary outside of the New Testament Gospels is the *Dialogue of the Savior*, a fragmented text from the Nag Hammadi library that may have its origin in the first century. Although there is no mention of a sexual relationship between Jesus and Mary, there's no doubt that Mary was one of Jesus's pet students. Whereas the canonical Gospels indicate that Peter, John, and James were closest to the Savior, this apocryphal text suggests just the opposite—that Jesus's three most intimate disciples were his twin brother Judas Thomas, a man called Matthew, and the precocious Mary Magdalene. This secret scripture proceeds to explain that Mary was "a woman who understood everything," and that she had frequent conversations with her Savior, the latter of whom suggested that she and the others would "be blessed when you strip off your clothing. For there is no great thing [to lay aside] what is external."[12]

It's difficult to know exactly what to make of strange statements like these, but there is a more controversial apocryphal text that has provided the most fodder for the claim that Jesus and Mary Magdalene were sexually intimate. Discovered at Nag Hammadi, this second- or third-century *Gospel of Philip* states that "Three women always walked with the master: Mary his

The second-century *Gospel of Mary* is another fascinating, though fragmentary, Gnostic text. Discovered in the nineteenth century, it contains a private revelation Jesus gave his favorite disciple, Mary Magdalene. The text ends with Mary arguing with Peter (something common in other Gnostic texts), and Levi calling Peter to task, "if the Savior made [Mary] worthy, who are you then for your part to reject her? Assuredly the Savior's knowledge of her is completely reliable. That is why he loved her more than us."[23]

mother, [his] sister, and Mary of Magdala, who is called his companion."[13] Several chapters later this cryptic gospel elaborates on what "companion"—a term based on the Greek word for "associate" or "partner"—may have meant:

> The companion of the [Savior] is Mary of Magdala. The [Savior loved] her more than [all] the disciples, [and he] kissed her often on her [mouth]. The other [disciples]...said to him, 'Why do you love her more than all of us?' The Savior answered and said to them, 'Why don't I love you like her? If a blind person and one who can see are both in darkness, they are the same. When the light comes, one who can see will see the light, and the blind person will stay in darkness.' (64)

Even though this passage is chock-full of word gaps (indicated by brackets) and unclear in the original Coptic source, this has not deterred detective novelists and armchair historians from vocalizing the sexual innuendo between Jesus and his most notorious female disciple. What scholars see as unrecoverable gaps to an intriguing yet unclear story, conspiracy theorists see as clear evidence of sexual foul play. Like it or not, however, there is no text in existence—apocryphal or not—indicating *explicitly* that Jesus and Mary Magdalene were illicit lovers or even lawfully abiding spouses. This includes the so-called *Gospel of Jesus's Wife*, a fragment purporting to teach that Jesus and Mary were married, which has been proven a forgery. And when it comes to the document discussed above, slanderer of Christianity Bart Ehrman argues that even if the *Gospel of Philip* did indicate that Jesus used to kiss Mary on the mouth, "it is not a prelude to sex. It is a symbolic statement that [Mary] received the revelation of truth that [Jesus] conveyed to [all of] his disciples."[14]

JESUS'S SECRET DISCIPLE: THE *GOSPEL OF JUDAS*

But historically sane responses to sensationally based claims have hardly convinced revisionists and conspiracy theorists. According to them, Mary Magdalene *was* Jesus's lover. Thomas *was* Jesus's twin brother. And Judas *was* Jesus's misunderstood ally. This last claim—in many ways the boldest and bravest to date—is highly popular today. Far from betraying his Savior in a cosmic act of self-interest, we are told, Judas the Betrayer was the only one of Jesus's disciples who truly understood him. Discovered in Egypt in the late twentieth century, the *Gospel of Judas* ignited a fire of controversy when it was released to the public in 2006 for suggesting that Judas was Jesus's most faithful companion.

This second-century gospel, like so many other Gnostic scriptures, presents us with an enchantingly curious opening line: "The secret revelatory discourse that Jesus spoke with Judas Iscariot in the course of a week, three days before his passion."[15] According to this gospel, Jesus often appeared to his disciples in the form a child. He was also fond of laughing,

First Page of *The Gospel of Judas*. Courtesy of WolfgangRieger.

something that none of the four canonical Gospels ever record Jesus to have done (though, of course, he would have). Problem was, however, that the disciples were usually the butt of Jesus's jokes in the *Gospel of Judas*. Of the disciples, Judas Iscariot was the only one who could apparently "stand before"[16] the imposing Jesus, and he was also the only one who truly understood where Jesus came from and what he came to accomplish. In the Bizarro World of Apocryphal Christianity, Judas's confession of faith stands as a direct contrast to Peter's in the New Testament. Whereas Peter confesses to Jesus in the Gospel of Matthew, "You are the Messiah, the Son of the living God" (Matt. 16:16), Judas professes the following in the *Gospel of Judas*: "You have come from the immortal realm [or eon] of Barbelo."[17] From what realm or eon? From Barbelo—that's the divine mother according to other Gnostic texts such as the *Secret Book of John*, a product of Sethian Christians groups that were popular in the second and third centuries.

After answering in the *Gospel of Judas* that Jesus came from Barbelo, Jesus told his prized disciple Judas to leave the remaining eleven disciples in

"The Father gazed into Barbelo, with the pure light surrounding the Invisible Spirit...Barbelo conceived from him, and he produced a spark of light similar to the blessed light but not as great. This was the only child of the Mother-Father that had come forth, the only offspring, the only Child of the Father, the pure light...The holy Spirit brought the divine Self-Generated Child of himself and Barbelo to perfection, so that the Child might stand before the great Invisible Virgin Spirit as the divine Self-Generated, the anointed."[24]

order to become "the thirteenth spirit." Judas acquiesced, but found that his special relationship with Jesus made him the source of misunderstanding and even persecution. Jesus reassured Judas, however, that even though he would be "cursed by the other generations [of Christians]...eventually you will rule over them."[18] Not a bad fate for someone the New Testament describes as a thief and a vehicle of Satan. The *Gospel of Judas* ends with Jesus teaching his star pupil how [Judas] will be liberating Jesus's spirit from [Jesus's] flesh by turning [Jesus] over to the authorities. As Jesus confides to Judas, "you will exceed all of [the other disciples by turning me in]. For you will sacrifice the man [that clothes] me."[19] According to the standard argument of conspiracy theorists, this passage unequivocally proves that Judas was the real hero of the Christian story, for he alone understood that Jesus's betrayal was necessary in order for Jesus to return to the heavenly realm. Far from betraying his Lord for thirty pieces of silver, Judas simply followed the secret game plan that his Master had concocted through the course of their private conversations and revealed to him before Jesus's death. It was a story so dazzling to believe that it had to be buried deep into the recesses of the earth.

The Kiss of Judas **by Giotto di Bondone.**

WHO WANTS TO BE AN IGNORAMUS?

But not all that glitters is gold. As alluring as apocryphal documents like the *Gospel of Judas* appear to modern readers disenfranchised with brick-and-mortar, sin-and-damnation Christianity, they were as widely known as they were collectively panned by early church authorities. Far from encouraging mainstream leaders to look at tried-and-true stories with open-minded hearts, apocryphal texts became the bane of their existence. Irenaeus, a second-century bishop in modern France, denounced the *Gospel of Judas* for indulging in fanciful exaggeration. With a broader target in sight, Jerome, the celebrated Bible translator and crotchety early intellectual, wrote that "the devil insidiously resides in the apocrypha with his preciosities, in order to devour the innocent." In gleeful sarcasm, he amused himself that "the lullabies of the apocrypha ought to be sung rather to dead heretics than to living ecclesiastics," and that "there are many ignoramuses who follow the absurdities of the apocrypha and even prefer these lullabies to the authentic books."[20]

Jerome couldn't anticipate how right he was—though it's doubtful that anyone would appreciate being called an ignoramus. With the publication of "secret scriptures" and "hidden gospels" widely and wildly circulating among curious readers today, there's a whole segment of society enthralled with the idea that the apocryphal books are more authentic versions of Christianity than the books that eventually came to be included in the New Testament. There is every indication to believe that these rival interpretations of traditional Christianity are here to stay. The older the ancient document—and the more outrageous and exaggerated—the better. It makes little difference to many modern readers that such documents tell us next to nothing about the historical Jesus or, for that matter, the historical Judas, Thomas, Philip, Mary Magdalene, Paul, or Peter.

ENDNOTES

1 This story only exists now in the writings of Eusebius, the early church historian and bishop of Caesarea. See his *The History of the Church* 6.12, trans. G. A. Williamson (London: Penguin, 1989), 190.

2 Leo, "Letter 15," modified from Rose, *Ritual Memory: The Apocryphal Acts and Liturgical Commemoration in the Early Medieval West (c. 500-1215)* (Leiden, the Netherlands: Brill, 2009), 47.

3 Philastrius, *Liber de Haeresibus*, Patrologia Latina col. 88, p. 1200.

4 Innocentius I, "Epistula 6.7," in Rose, *Ritual Memory*, 47.

5 Quoted in Hans-Josef Klauck, *Apocryphal Gospels: An Introduction*, trans. Brian McNeil (London and New York: T&T Clark International, 2003), 5.

6 Rose, *Ritual Memory*, 25.

7 Rose, *Ritual Memory*, 27.

8 Proto-Gospel of James 20:1," in *After the New Testament: A Reader in Early Christianity*, ed. Bart Ehrman (New York and Oxford: Oxford University Press, 1999) 253.

9 "The Infancy Gospel of Thomas 3:2," in *After the New Testament*, 256.

10 "The Infancy Gospel of Thomas 9:3," in *After the New Testament*, 257.

11 "The Gospel of Thomas with the Greek Gospel of Thomas," in *The Nag Hammadi Scriptures: The International Edition*, ed. Marvin Meyer (New York: HarperCollins, 2007), 139.

12 "The Dialogue of the Savior 139 and 143," in *The Nag Hammadi Scriptures*, 308, 310. Brackets indicate gaps in the original text, lost due to the sands of time. Most likely, the stripping away of clothes is not at all a sexual reference but one relating to the stripping away of physical things and putting on the clothes of secret or higher wisdom.

13 "The Gospel of Philip 59," in *The Nag Hammadi Scriptures*, 167.

14 Bart Ehrman, *Peter, Paul, and Mary Magdalene: The Followers of Jesus in History and Legend* (Oxford: Oxford University Press, 2006), 216.

15 "The Gospel of Judas 33," in *The Nag Hammadi Scriptures*, 760.

16 "The Gospel of Judas 34," in *The Nag Hammadi Scriptures*, 761.

17 "The Gospel of Judas 34 ," in *The Nag Hammadi Scriptures*, 761.

18 "The Gospel of Judas 44 and 46," in *The Nag Hammadi Scriptures*, 764, 765.

19 "The Gospel of Judas 56 ," in *The Nag Hammadi Scriptures*, 768.

20 Quoted in Rose, *Ritual Memory*, 50–51.

21 N. T. Wright, *Judas and the Gospel of Jesus* (London: SPCK, 2009), 9.

22 "Pistis Sophia 36 and 122," in Bart Ehrman, *Jesus, Peter, and Mary Magdalene*, 209–210.

23 "*The Gospel of Mary* 18," in *The Nag Hammadi Scriptures*, 745.

24 *Secret Book of John* 6-7," in *The Nag Hammadi Scriptures*, 111–112.

Chapter 8

SERVING GOD AND MONEY

He was at it again. For years as the leading preacher in the historically Christian city of Antioch, John "Golden-mouth" (*Chrysostom* in Greek) had mesmerized churchgoers with his booming self-confidence, stunning rhetoric, rhythmic voice, and prophetic critique of the rich. It was not at all uncommon for his sermons to be interrupted by applause, and one historian has gone so far as to assert that John Chrysostom is the most acclaimed Christian preacher of all time.[1] In fact, John had become so famous as a preacher in Antioch that he was hastily ordered to become the bishop of Constantinople when that prestigious office was vacated in 397. From the point of view of emperor Arcadius and his wife empress Eudoxia, the best city in the world should have the best orator.

But Constantinople was no Antioch. Built by emperor Constantine in the year 330 as the new Rome—*Nova Roma*—Constantinople was the capital of the Roman Empire and the residence of its most prominent and wealthy citizens, including the imperial family. Though only seventy years old, this new city had quickly inherited the complex political machinery of ancient Rome as well as the glaring disparities between rich and poor. As church historian Justo González explains, "Most members of the court [in Constantinople] were rich absentee landowners… [who] spent prodigally on luxuries, extravagant feasts, and sumptuous residences. Meanwhile, the vast majority of the permanent population lived in wretched tenements…[and] had been uprooted by the land-grabbing greed of the powerful."[2] The disparity between the two groups was too much for John Goldenmouth to stomach. What else should we expect from a man who made a name for himself in Antioch for preaching that refusal "to share our own wealth with

***John Chrysostom Confronting Empress Aelia Eudoxia* by Jean-Paul Laurens.**

the poor is theft" and that "Countless poor people have to go hungry so that you can wear a single ruby"?[3]

Now in the crucible of Constantinople, perched on his podium in full sight of the wealthy elite, John denounced extravagance, opulence, and economic injustice. He questioned prevailing attitudes about ownership of land, and he exhorted the rich to be generous in almsgiving and merciful to the poor. He was, in the words of one great historian, "the master-preacher of charity."[4] In his biblically fused preaching, John openly contrasted the chains of servitude, which the apostle Paul wore around his body, to the gold and splendor that the empress had draped around hers.[5] He even reportedly compared the empress to the leading female villains in the Bible: to Jezebel, the murderer of innocent Naboth in the Old Testament; and to Herodias, the murderer of innocent John the Baptist in the New. Needless to say, it did not take Eudoxia long before she "had come to loathe Chrysostom personally,"[6] feeling like the most famous preacher alive was continually pointing his judgmental finger at her every action. In 402, Eudoxia finally got her husband to banish Bishop John from the imperial city, though he was almost immediately reinstalled after a devastating earthquake occurred the very night he was fired, leading the imperial court to wonder if God was displeased with their actions. Unfortunately for John, the only subsequent earthquakes that erupted came from his sermons, and he was almost immediately exiled to the far reaches of eastern Turkey, where he died en route to an even more remote location of exile in 407.

THE RISK OF REPROACHING THE RICH

It was a risky business to criticize the wealthy in the heart of imperial Christianity. Golden-mouth or not, though, John didn't particularly care. Well aware of the strong injunctions for the care of widows, foreigners, and orphans in the Old Testament, as well as the attention on charity and good works in the New, John preached unwaveringly on these themes. The letters of Paul and the other apostles were nothing if they were not epistles embedded with exhortations to provide for widows, enhance the plight of the poor, and generally ensure the welfare of the Christian faithful. The loss of his job for preaching against greed and economic injustice revealed

Expulsion of the Money-changers from the Temple **by Giotto di Bondone.**

just how much Christianity had evolved since its formation in the first century, at which point the Christian religion was not at all rich. Despite reports from some contemporary sources that Christians were distinguished from pagans in their care for the poor, not all that glittered in the ancient Christian world was gold. During Christianity's temptation with social respectability between the third and fifth centuries, in particular, it sometimes confused God with goods and worship with wealth. Taking Jesus's saying that "you cannot serve both God and money" (Matt. 6:24) back to the cutting board of interpretation, Christians pondered whether religion and riches might not be so incompatible after all.

NO CASH IN HIS KNAPSACK: JESUS AND WEALTH

Although Jesus was not allergic to money, he kept it at a distance. He nonchalantly accepted the contributions of wealthy women that accompanied him, but there are no examples in the Gospels that he ever carried cash in his knapsack. When confronted with the drudgeries of a poll-tax in Galilee, for instance, Jesus encouraged Peter to seek the money in the mouth of a fish (Matt. 17:24–27). When scribes and chief priests inquired whether it was appropriate for pious Jews to pay taxes to pagan Romans, Jesus made an object lesson out of them by making *them* present a denarius inside the Temple (Matt. 22:15–22). And when it was supper time in Galilee and thousands of his audience were without food, Jesus performed a miracle of bread and fish rather than pulling out a wad of dough (Matt. 14:13–21). It is more than ironic that the only one of Jesus's disciples to betray him was the one who carried money: Judas.

Jesus's teachings and parables were rich with warnings about riches. They borrowed heavily from the economic realities of his day—tapping into a world replete with landowners, field workers, slaves, stewards, riches, wages, wine, clothing, food, and taxes. Jesus's actual sayings about wealth are legendary. He taught onlookers that it is "easier for a camel to pass through the eye of a needle than it is for a rich person to enter the kingdom of heaven" (Matt. 19:24). He advised his followers not to "store up... treasures on earth" but to invest imperishable goods in heaven (6:19). He taught a would-be disciple to "sell your possessions and give to the poor" in order to truly be perfect (19:21). He said "woe to you who are rich" (Luke 6:24), "be on your guard against all kinds of greed" (12:15), and "blessed are you who are poor" (6:20). Other than the kingdom of God, wealth was one of the topics that Jesus addressed most during his short ministry on earth. It was, in fact, one of the primary reasons he was crucified. In Jerusalem, just days before being arrested by the Jewish elite, Jesus "overturned the tables of the money changers" and disparaged the Temple system for being a "den or robbers" rather than a "house of prayer" (Matt. 21:12–13). When the wealthy members of the Jewish Sanhedrin delivered Jesus to the Roman governor Pontius Pilate for execution, their silver bullet of incrimination was Jesus's teaching on wealth: "we found this man perverting our nation, forbidding us to pay taxes to the emperor" (Luke 23:12).

SAVING THE RICH, FEEDING THE POOR

That was no small charge within the Roman Empire. It was one thing to perform miracles in the backwaters of Galilee among Jewish peasants, but altogether different to put a clog in the wheel of Roman commerce. It's arguable whether Christianity ever would have become a world religion had it kept to its strict positions on wealth. Truth is, one could argue that not even Jesus's ministry would have taken off had there not been people of means willing to finance it. The Gospel of Luke clearly reports that Jesus and his disciples were financially supported by "Mary, called Magdalene…and Joanna, the wife of Herod's steward Chuza, and Susanna, *and many others*, who provided for them out of their [own] resources" (Luke 8:2–3). Religious cults had come and gone in the Roman Empire, but those that withstood the test of time played by common rules. If Christianity was going to go far and wide, it had to go deep into the patterns of society. It had to pay tribute to the customs of the age. It had to respect the rich.

> From its beginning, and continuing for centuries, Christianity "attracted a disproportionate number of higher-status women compared to aristocratic men."[47]

But what if respecting the rich could be a means of providing for the poor? According to the *Sybilline Oracles*, a collection of Christian books written in the first centuries after Christ, the age to come would be a utopian wonderland where "wealth will have no division" and where everyone "will be on a par together."[7] Much of early Christian apocalyptic literature ached for an end to earthly distinctions between the wealthy and the poor, the high born and the low born, the haves and the have-nots. Written in the second century, the apocalyptic *Shepherd of Hermas* understood earthly wealth to make one "useless" before God.[8] While lost-in-thought apocalypticists daydreamed about the destruction of the rich in the age to come, however, more sober-minded Christian leaders wondered how the Christian rich of earth might contribute to the kingdom of heaven.

Cyprian of Carthage, a third-century bishop living in the wealthiest city after Rome, knew how to combine commerce with Christianity. A savvy and affluent nobleman with a penchant for pragmatism, his brief career as bishop was forged in the crucible of persecution. One of the most pressing issues he encountered as bishop revolved around what to do with Christians under his care who denied their faith during persecution but who wanted to snuggle up to Mother Church after persecution ended. Not surprising given that they had the most to lose, it was the wealthy who were especially susceptible to this sin of apostasy. Recognizing their need to do penance on the one hand and the growing financial needs of the church on the other, Cyprian attempted to kill two birds with one stone. In his book *Works and Almsgiving*, written in the 250s, Bishop Cyprian argued that prosperous penitent apostates could expiate their sins by writing a check to the bishop. Though conceding that Christ's death secured salvation, Cyprian insisted that almsgiving "safeguard[ed]" it. Drawing richly from the Old Testament Apocryphal book of Tobit, he taught that "by almsgiving souls are freed from death." Because earthly wealth made one poor "in the sight of God," Cyprian encouraged the rich to cede their fortunes to him so that they could become "coheir[s] of [Christ's] heavenly kingdom."[9] Like making lemonade out of lemons, Cyprian was all too aware, notes one commentator, of how "the flow of alms helped bridge social fissures"[10] within his community.

KEEPING THE WEALTHY IN THEIR PLACE

Cyprian's harmonizing of the rich with the poor in his churches was brilliantly orchestrated. The ancients were nothing if they were not class-conscious. As historian of early Christianity Helen Rhee underscores, "Roman society was obsessed with maintaining social distinctions and hierarchy."[11] Every person fell into a predefined pecking order and was expected to play his or her part within the social pyramid of life. Christianity hadn't changed that. The apostle Paul, for instance, had battled through such social divisions in the churches that he oversaw in the houses of aristocrats across the Mediterranean basin in the first century. The distinctions among senatorial families, equestrians, decurions, plebs, and slaves had been cemented ages before. This edifice would not crumble easily, if at all. Everyone knew that it was the duty of higher classes (patrons) to provide food, bathhouses, aqueducts, entertainment (through plays, games, and chariot races), physical protection, dinner invitations, and jobs to lower classes (clients), just as it was the duty of clients to enhance their patrons' honor and social standing by providing votes at election time, making daily house visits, and praising them in public settings. It was a highly effective, though utterly undemocratic, system that fit ancient society like a misshapen glove.

When wealthy Christians started to enter the church more consistently in the third and fourth centuries, these social distinctions weren't at all obliterated. They were merely "modified."[12] Far from requiring rich Christians to sell their earthly possessions and take up the cross of poverty, bishops allowed them to maintain their highfalutin social status in exchange for exclusive patronage rights. As we saw with Cyprian, this was a win-win situation, for it provided for the spiritual *and* material needs of the Christian community. It's no wonder that when civil officials during the Great Persecution of 303 ransacked the holdings of a local church in North Africa, they found more shoes than Scriptures. Among other items discovered, officials confiscated "82 women's tunics, 38 capes, 16 men's tunics, 13 pairs of men's shoes, 47 pairs of women's shoes, [and] 19 peasant clasps."[13] Churches were not just houses of worship, they were centers of distributions. And the rich now attending these churches made such distributions possible. Though there were clear exceptions, many Christian bishops were unwilling to bite the hands that fed them. On the contrary, it was bishops who profited most from this ecclesiastical enterprise since they were the ones who gained prominence, prestige, and power.[14]

The arrival of so many wealthy men and women into church settings naturally altered the content of sermons. Apparently, from the fourth century onward, a veritable theology of "'redemptive almsgiving' [became] one of the most consistent elements in the sermons and teachings of church leaders."[15] With astonishing alacrity, bishops took to the task of persuading rich folks that building basilicas, furnishing churches, subsidizing monasteries, commissioning works of theology, and providing money for the Christian poor was not just good for their soul—it was also redemptive. Bishop Augustine, taking full aim at the age-old practice of civic benefaction, preached that rich Christians who funded public games rather than church ministries were to be "condemned, rebuked, and changed for the better."[16] His contemporary Bishop Gaudentius of Brescia was even bolder. When a rich man in his parish thought God was punishing him with sickness for being so fabulously wealthy, Gaudentius replied: "God ha[s] not made you rich out of ill-will but providentially, so that you should find a medicine to heal your sins through works of mercy."[17]

> The term *euergetism* ("doing good deeds" in Greek) refers to the obligation in the ancient world of wealthy citizens to use their personal wealth to fund shows, games, special events, and construction projects for the good of their community. When wealthy Romans began entering the church, the task of the bishop was not to convince the rich to give, but to give to the right cause—to the church. The existence today of so many churches, basilicas, convents, and monasteries from the ancient world shows how successful they were.

CHRISTIANITY, CONSTANTINE, AND CASH

Emperor Constantine, though by no means the first wealthy Christian, was the first of unquestionable prominence to patron the church. His "works of mercy" have rippled throughout the ages, splashing into our laps even to this day. Though frequently overlooked among church historians, there was one purely material act that Constantine did that paid huge spiritual dividends for the body of Christ. Three years before coming under the protection of the Christian God at the Battle of the Milvian

Bridge (312), twelve years before making Sunday a holiday for his new client religion (321), and sixteen years before convening the Council of Nicea (325), Constantine (re-)created a new form of currency. The Roman *solidus* was so-called because it was nothing less than a solid drop of precious gold. Molded into a circle of 4.5 grams, the *solidus* stabilized the Roman economy that minted the way for the golden era of church architecture and Christian patronage.[18] The gold now sprinkled on page leafs from Bibles, adorned inside magnificent basilicas, and coated on ever-present crosses was connected to the currency of Christianity's greatest patron.

Constantine's issuance of gold coins could not have come at a better time for the Christian Church. In 313, a mere four years after Constantine began minting this new currency, the historically momentous Edict of Milan was issued. Besides granting Christians freedom of worship across the empire, this edict ordered all former church property to be restored "immediately...by energetic action...without any delay."[19] As if to make the fine point on the edict even clearer, Constantine hastily followed it with a spate of letters to Christian leaders promising them lumps of cold, hard cash. Writing in the year 313 to Bishop Caecilian of Carthage, Constantine guaranteed the blessed bishop "3,000 folles in cash,"[20] an incredibly large sum of money. He made similar pledges to other bishops and gave tax exemptions to the clergy. And in the Eternal City of the empire, Rome, he donated two basilicas to the church: Saint Peter's on Vatican Hill and Saint John Lateran, both of which endure today as the headquarters of the Roman Catholic Church and of the Diocese of Rome, respectively.[21] Whereas Christianity had formerly been "invisible"[22] in Rome, even as late as the early fourth century, it was now seen by all, impossible to be overlooked, and growing richer with every Roman minute.

Patronage of the church by Constantine and his successors naturally accelerated Christianity's growth. It also put paganism's religious lease on notice. Just as the church was becoming the apple of the emperors' eye, pagan shrines were being despoiled by the dozens. Although the imperial family owned the mines needed to extract enough of the precious metal to spread the fiscal love, Christian emperors from the time of Constantine onward began looting pagan shrines for any vestiges of gold they could find. As they "spoiled the Egyptians," as it were, churchgoers whooped in delight. They savored the destruction of pagan shrines

> "The great patronized Christianity, but they did not necessarily take part in the life of the local churches. In maintaining this distance they followed the example of their emperor. Though acclaimed as the first Christian emperor, Constantine was never seen in a Christian church outside his palace. Emperors only began to attend church services in public after his death in 337."[48]

like a fine glass of Spanish sherry by a wine connoisseur. As fourth-century Christian aristocrat Julius Firmicus Maternus exclaimed:

> Take away, yes, calmly take away, Most Holy Emperors, the adornments of the [pagan] temples. Let the fire of the mint or the blaze of the smelters melt them down, and confiscate all the votive offerings to your own use and ownership.[23]

Even though such gold technically fell under the purview of the emperor's budget line, it was what Constantine did with the gold that upset so many pagan critics. Commenting several generations after Constantine's time, the pagan historian Zosimus reproached the emperor for "wasting revenue by unnecessary gifts to unworthy and useless people…enriching those who were useless to the state."[24] The "unworthy and useless people" Zosimus was referring to were no longer "the dregs of society," as Marcus Cornelius Fronto labeled this religious lot in the second century; quite the reverse, they were fast becoming the societal cream of the crop—Christians. And with each new passing decade, they were becoming more respectable and richer still. In addition to imperial funds now being funneled into the bishop's coffers and doles of grain being dished out to their dioceses, Constantine gave legal permission in 321 for bequests to be given to the church upon a person's death—a great boon to the church's annual budget. The "overall impact" of this lavish patronage upon the church has been described as "nothing less than revolutionary."[25]

THE BIBLE COSTS HOW MUCH?

Whatever it was, it was changing the very character of Christianity. "To many Roman aristocrats," explains classicist Cynthia White, "the church's growing wealth, power, and social exclusivity appealed as much as any religious doctrine, and this status appeal accounted for the 'religious' conversion of many Roman aristocrats."[26] One of the most important contributions that aristocratic Christians made was in the form of books. Unlike the modern world, which takes books (whether digital or print) completely for granted, they were "stunningly expensive" in the an-

> Although Christians did not invent codices (modern-day books), they adapted them faster than anyone else. Christians made use of codices because they were cheaper than rolls (or scrolls), could be written double-sided, could be read using only one hand, and were easier to store (or hide). Not surprisingly, by the fourth century, the codex had become "the accepted and almost exclusive form for New Testament manuscripts."[49]

cient world.[27] Not only were books difficult to obtain, but they had to be painstakingly copied by hand before the creation of the printing press in the fifteenth century. At a time when only ten percent of the population could read, historian Megan Williams estimates that extensive use of books was restricted "to between 1 and 5 percent"[28] of the population, meaning that the books historians utilize to reconstruct Christian history were the products of the absolute highest echelons of intellectual society. The dissemination of knowledge across the ancient world, in other words, was about money—and mountains of it. It's not surprising that a wealth of Christian literature flooded the marketplace of ancient society around the time of Constantine. Without too much exaggeration, the distribution of knowledge was often by fiat of fat-cat aristocrats—the only class of people in the ancient world wealthy enough to commission and sustain such a large circulation of intellectual property.

The dissemination of information naturally included the *magnum opus* of the Christian life—the *Verbum Dei*, or "Word of God." Despite its overabundance today, the likes of which can be found in the drawer of any lackluster hotel room, a Bible in the ancient world was ridiculously rare. Its scarcity can be attributed not just to desperately low levels of literacy—what's the point of making books nobody can read?—but also cost. Peter Brown estimates that "Each copy of the Gospels alone cost as much as a marble sarcophagus."[29] In other words, the cost of a Bible was the same as a casket—and a deluxe version one at that. And as Alex Trebek is wont to inform us in commercials as we watch nighttime television, a casket—let alone a funeral in general—can cost thousands.

Sarcophagus of *Patronus* with Slave Holding Book by Giovanni Dall'Orto.

For a man who had unrivaled access to magnificent libraries across the world, and whose yearly salary would have otherwise made a personal library a fairytale, the biblical scholar Jerome was surprisingly critical of the costly production of books. Writing a letter in the year 385 to the daughter of his most faithful patroness, Jerome bemoaned: "Parchment is dyed purple, gold is melted to make letters…, codices are clothed in gems, and the naked Christ dies outside their doors."[30] Like it or not, the types of expensive books to which Jerome was likely referring are the best examples remaining of Bibles from the ancient world. In fact, the oldest surviving manuscript containing Jerome's Latin translation of the

Bible—called Codex Amiatinus, produced in a monastery in England—was splendidly illuminated, masterfully decorated, and ridiculously cost-prohibitive. Medieval historian Frans van Liere estimates that it would have taken around five hundred sheep or calves simply to produce the parchment needed for the precious book, let alone the cost of labor and other materials.[31]

We can also see how wealth, literacy, and religion fused in the famous library of Caesarea, a coastal city in modern Israel where the church historian Eusebius became bishop in the year 314. Thanks to the personal fortune of a Christian man named Pamphilus, the library at Caesarea boasted one of the largest collections in all of antiquity. Such an assortment of books, however, "would have been available only to those at the pinnacle of the social pyramid, or through their patronage."[32] Because he was an intellectual as well as the bishop of this important city, Eusebius received unfettered access to this treasure-trove of books, which included copies of the Bible, of Origen's work

> One of Origen's most important works was the Hexapla, a Bible in six versions. The manufacture of such an expensive book would have been impossible without the incredible wealth of patrons. The writing of this book—including labor, scribes, and materials—would have cost 155,000 denarii, the equivalent of several years of a teacher's salary.[50]

Ancient City of Caesarea Maritima, Israel. Courtesy of DerHexer.

(who lived in Caesarea toward the end of his life), and of other expensive books to which many other Christians had no access. With such a grand collection at his disposal, it's no wonder that Eusebius is the single best source for any historical reconstruction of the first three centuries of the church. However, if it weren't for the incredible wealth that funded the library at Caesarea—as well as other libraries Eusebius frequented in his travels—we would be even more in the dark than we are about what happened in the church's past. As the saying goes, "money matters."

DEEP POCKETS AND DEEP PHILOSOPHERS

This same sentiment applies, of course, to two of the most prolific authors of the early church: Jerome and Augustine. It's a little-recognized fact that these scholars' achievements, writings, and legacies were completely dependent upon the patronage of wealthier, aristocratic men and women. Stated more bluntly, "Patronage was a fact of life."[33] In the Roman Empire there were no self-made men. Behind the careers of even the most innovative of thinkers were moneyed persons with deep, deep pockets. This is nothing to be embarrassed by. Years before Christian institutions had the resources available to fund the work of independent scholars—or before printing presses could mass market millions of best-sellers—being a client to a wealthy patron or patroness was the surest means to a life of leisurely study. It was, in all likelihood, the only way.

The great scholar Jerome was a client of multiple patrons and patronesses throughout his illustrious career. In fact, Jerome's very translation of the Latin Vulgate, "the single most important text in western Christendom,"[34] was made possible by the patronage of, among others, Pope Damasus in Rome (until his death in 384) and Paula in Bethlehem, who endowed his monastic residences in the Holy Land and provided the materials and labor needed to continue the massive translational undertaking. Paula's patronage in Bethlehem was the wind in Jerome's sails for two decades, though Jerome was always looking through his telescope for additional financial supporters. Despite living in a cave in the middle of nowhere, he still had to keep up appearances. In the preface to his translation of Proverbs, Ecclesiastes, and the Song of Songs in the year 398, Jerome later acknowledged and thanked the patronage of two prominent bishops: "You sent us the consolation of money, you have supported our secretaries and our scribes, so that by your assistance our ability might toil the more."[35] Jerome, a "provincial upstart" who had excelled at forming ties with a small "circle of aristocratic Christians,"[36] was always aware of the economic realities before him. Up until his death in 419, patronage shaped what he wrote, to whom he wrote, and why he wrote. This teaches us an important lesson from history: Although we like to envision the great writers of the faith responding to this or that topic based on the prompting of the Spirit, it was just as often the whims of moneyed patrons dictating whether scholars could afford to write at all, let alone whether they could write theological tractates, commentaries, letters, or even biblical translations.[37] As with so many other writers during his generation, "Jerome's scholarship and the dissemination of his works depended…[on] the late Roman elite."[38]

Though hundreds of miles away by sea, Augustine was in the same boat as Jerome. Like the prolific monk from the Balkans, Augustine was an ambitious scholastic from Roman Africa who depended on the wealthy of the world to make a name for himself. "More than anyone else in the ancient world," one historian notes, "Augustine can be characterized by his constant and intensive preoccupation with books."[39] But in order to live in the realm of books, he had to first make it in the realm of patronage. And that's exactly what he did. "From the early 370s up to the time of his conversion in 386…Augustine's career depended at every stage on the patronage of others."[40] Such patronage first came through the likes of Romanianus, a wealthy man from Augustine's hometown of Thagaste (in present-day Algeria). It was Romanianus who bankrolled Augustine for twelve years while he was a wet-behind-the-ears and a not-much-in-his-knapsack professor in Thagaste and then in Carthage. According to Augustine, Romanianus had taken "this poor young boy" into "his house, his payroll and his heart."[41]

> "Patronage from a pope…not only guaranteed a scholar sufficient income and leisure to work, but it also made it more likely that his labors would be met with a favourable reception."[51]

When in Rome, after about a decade of teaching in North Africa, Augustine came under the patronage of a wildly wealthy and well-connected aristocrat named Symmachus. As a client of Symmachus, the city prefect,

Saint Augustine Taken to School by Saint Monica **by Nicolo di Pietro.**

Augustine was duty-bound to daily visit his home despite a full teaching load and time spent reading. It might have been during one of these daily visits that Augustine first heard that Symmachus had selected Augustine—of all the other talented Roman men—to receive one of the finest teaching posts in the entire Latin world: employment in Milan. But in Milan it was not so much what he taught—he actually didn't stay there incredibly long—but who he met. In the most fabulous city in northern Italy, Augustine came under the spellbinding sermons of Bishop Ambrose, who baptized Augustine in the year 387. Western Christianity's most famous and prolific child was now a Christian—and the providence of this act was beautifully orchestrated by pockets of pagan money.

WIDENING THE EYE OF THE NEEDLE

When Augustine later returned to his native Africa and eventually became bishop of the city of Hippo, there were plenty of wealthy people in his diocese. Fortunately for him, a policy on how to handle such rich people had been scripted ages ago. Writing in the late second century, Clement of Alexandria presented the earliest systematic exposition of the story of the Rich Young Ruler in a booklet entitled *Who Is the Rich Man Who Is Saved?* The occasion of Clement's booklet was the utter despair that wealthy Christians experienced upon hearing Jesus's bare-faced words that the rich would only be perfect after renouncing all of their possessions, unforgettably uttering that it would be "easier for a camel to go through the eye of a needle than for someone who is rich to enter the kingdom of God" (Matt. 19:24). With such an explosive passage threatening the very concept that rich Christians could be saved, the learned Clement turned to damage control. He was unwilling to part with wealthy would-be Christians—camels or not. He argued that the "hidden" meaning of Jesus's words were less about renouncing possessions and more about "renounc[ing] the passions."[42] "For salvation," he explained, was "the privilege of pure and passionless souls," not possession-less ones.[43] What exactly, he coolly reasoned, would be the point of Christian charity "if nobody had anything [to share]?"[44]

> The *salutatio* was a daily ritual in which Roman clients greeted their patrons in exchange for food, dinner invitations, or money. As a client, Augustine would have daily participated in the *salutatio*.

Clement's engagement with this deeply arresting passage was a watershed in early Christianity. According to historian of antiquity Elizabeth Clark, Clement's figurative interpretation was a "classic example of how a 'spiritualized' reading [of the Bible] might encourage a *weakening* of the ascetic rigor demanded by a more 'literal' exegesis."[45] By means of his allegorical method of interpretation, Clement hamstrung the plain meaning of one of the most galloping verses of Scripture. Rather than narrowing it, many ancient Christians like Clement concluded that it was preferable to widen the eye of the needle so that wealthy camels could mingle with the lambs at their leisure. Over time, with the advent of imperial Christianity during the time of Augustine, the amount of camels being smuggled through the ever-widening eye of the needle only increased, leading Peter Brown to christen this new epoch of the church as "the Age of the Camel."[46]

ENDNOTES

1 Justo González, *Faith and Wealth: A History of Early Christian Ideas on the Origin, Significance, and Use of Money* (San Francisco: Harper & Row, 1990), 200.

2 González, *Faith and Wealth*, 201.

3 Quoted in Francine Cardman, "Poverty and Wealth as Theater: John Chrysostom's Homilies on Lazarus and the Rich Man," and Rudolf Brandle, "The Sweetest Passage: Matthew 25:31–46 and Assistance to the Poor in the Homilies of John Chrysostom," in *Wealth and Poverty in Early Church and Society*, ed. Susan Holman (Grand Rapids, MI: Baker Academic, 2008), 172 and 100.

4 Peter Brown, *Poverty and Leadership in the Later Roman Empire* (Hanover, NH: University Press of New England, 2002), 64.

5 J. N. D. Kelly, *Golden Mouth: The Story of John Chrysostom: Ascetic, Preacher, Bishop* (Ithaca, NY: Cornell University Press, 1995), 150.

6 Philip Jenkins, *Jesus Wars: How Four Patriarchs, Three Queens, and Two Emperors Decided What Christians Would Believe for the Next 1,500 Years* (New York: HarperOne, 2011), 100.

7 "Sybilline Oracles 2:321-24," in *The Old Testament Pseudepigrapha*, vol. 1, *Apocalyptic Literature and Testaments*, ed. James Charlesworth (New York: Doubleday, 1983), 353.

8 "Shepherd of Hermas 14:7," in *The Apostolic Fathers*, 2nd ed., ed. Michael Holmes (Grand Rapids, MI: Baker, 1989), 205.

9 Cyprian, "Works and Almsgiving 1, 5, and 13," in *Saint Cyprian: Treatises*, vol. 36, *The Fathers of the Church: A New Translation*, ed. Roy Deferrari (Washington, DC: The Catholic University Press of America, 1958), 228, 232, 239.

10 Peter Brown, *"Through the Eye of a Needle": Wealth, the Fall of Rome, and the Making of Christianity in the West* (Princeton, NJ: Princeton University Press, 2012), 43.

11 Helen Rhee, *Loving the Poor, Saving the Rich: Wealth, Poverty, and Early Christian Formation* (Grand Rapids, MI: Baker Academic, 2012), 6.

12 Annewies van den Hoek, "Widening the Eye of the Needle: Wealth and Poverty in the Works of Clement of Alexandria," in *Wealth and Poverty*, 68.

13 *Christianity in the Later Roman Empire: A Sourcebook*, ed. David Gwynn (London: Bloomsbury Publishing, 2015), 185.

14 Brown, *Poverty and Leadership in the Later Roman Empire*, 45–73.

15 Rhee, *Loving the Poor, Saving the Rich*, 76.

16 Quoted in Brown, "*Through the Eye of a Needle*," 72.

17 Quoted in Brown, "*Through the Eye of a Needle*," 143.

18 Georges Depeyrot, "Economy and Society," in *The Cambridge Companion of the Age of Constantine*, ed. Noel Lenski (Cambridge: Cambridge University Press, 2005), 237.

19 Edict of Milan, quoted in Eusebius, *The History of the Church* 10.5, trans. G. A. Williamson (London: Penguin, 1995), 323.

20 Eusebius, *The History of the Church* 10.6, 326.

21 Naturally, the original edifices from the time of Constantine are gone, but the locations are unchanged.

22 Peter Brown, "*Through the Eye of a Needle*," 242.

23 Julius Firmicus Maternus, "De Errore Profanurum Religionum," in *Firmicus Maternus: The Error of the Pagan Religions*, trans. Clarence Forbes (New York, NY: Newman Press, 1970), 110.

24 Quoted in Depeyrot, "Economy and Society," *The Cambridge Companion*, 246.

25 Rhee, *Loving the Poor, Saving the Rich*, 179.

26 Cynthia White, *The Emergence of Christianity: Classical Traditions in Contemporary Perspective* (Minneapolis, MN: Fortress Press, 2011), 111.

27 Megan Hale Williams, *The Monk and the Book: Jerome and the Making of Christian Scholarship* (Chicago: University of Chicago Press, 2006), 174.

28 Williams, *The Monk and the Book*, 136.

29 Brown, "*Through the Eye of a Needle*," 275.

30 Jerome, Letter 22, quoted in Williams, *The Monk and the Book*, 181.

31 Frans van Liere, *An Introduction to the Medieval Bible* (Cambridge: Cambridge University Press, 2014), 9.

32 Williams, *The Monk and the Book*, 146.

33 Brown, "*Through the Eye of a Needle*," 25.

34 White, *The Emergence of Christianity*, 1145

35 Quoted in Williams, *The Monk and the Book*, 220.

36 Andrew Cain, *The Letters of Jerome: Asceticism, Biblical Exegesis, and the Construction of Christian Authority in Late Antiquity* (Oxford: Oxford University Press, 2009), 8.

37 Williams, *The Monk and the Book*, 247.

38 Williams, *The Monk and the Book*, 259.

39 Guy Stroumsa, "On the Status of Books in Early Christianity," in *Being Christian in Late Antiquity: A Festschrift for Gillian Clark*, ed. Carol Harrison et al. (Oxford: Oxford University Press, 2014), 69.

40 Brown, "*Through the Eye of a Needle*," 25.

41 Augustine, quoted in Brown, "*Through the Eye of a Needle*," 153.

42 Clement, "Who Is the Rich Man That Shall Be Saved 5 and 20," in *Ante-Nicene Fathers*, vol. 2, *Fathers of the Second Century: Hermas, Tatian, Athenagoras, Theophilus, and Clement of Alexandria*, ed. Alexander Roberts et al. (Grand Rapids, MI: Eerdmans, 1962), 592 and 596.

43 Clement, "Who Is the Rich Man 20," in *ANF* 2:596.

44 Clement, "Who Is the Rich Man 13," in *ANF* 2:594.

45 Elizabeth Clark, *Reading Renunciation: Asceticism and Scripture in Early Christianity* (Princeton, NJ: Princeton University Press, 1999), 94.

46 Brown, "*Through the Eye of a Needle*," xxiv.

47 Rhee, *Loving the Poor, Saving the Rich*, 134.

48 Brown, "*Through the Eye of a Needle*," 286.

49 Arthur Patzia, *The Making of the New Testament* (Downers Grove, IL: Intervarsity Press), 203.

50 Williams, *The Monk and the Book*, 175.

51 Cain, *The Letters of Jerome*, 48.

Chapter 9

PUTTING SEX ON TRIAL—GENDER AND RELIGION

Like countless other monks living in the ancient world, he more closely resembled a wandering homeless person than a Christian theologian. Gaunt and pale, Jovinian was eking out a humble existence on the meager rations of bread and water. Smelly and barefoot, he hobbled about in a black monastic tunic that was caked with dirt, residue, and Lord knows what else. Unmarried and celibate, he had renounced all the pleasures of sex and the enjoyment of a helpmate. Despite all appearances, however, Jovinian was a rising star among the galaxy of ancient Christian leaders. He was living the ancient Christian dream—self-denial, poverty, and celibacy. He was also gathering quite the following. There was not much more an ancient Christian could ask for.

But that's when fate turned against him. Jovinian decided to go public with his conviction that living on bread and water was not so glamorous after all, and that there wasn't anything wrong with eating a nice juicy steak every once a while, or consenting to the hygienic benefits of a *balneum*, or Roman bathhouse. Most appallingly, Jovinian used biblical passages to support the scandalous idea that virginity was not superior to marriage. Though remaining celibate himself, he taught that abstinence from sex did not make one a better Christian in God's sight. He taught that baptism in Christ imbued every person with the same amount of spiritual worth. He taught that God gave men and women the bonds of attraction and the organs of reproduction for a reason. He had to be stopped.

Not surprising given the sacrosanct status of celibacy in the late fourth century, "official ecclesiastical response to Jovinian was swift and unambiguous."[1] The greatest theologians of the day pounced on the lowly monk like he was peddling drugs, or at least pirating copies of the Gospels. In a scathing treaty, Jerome denounced Jovinian as "the Epicurus of the Christians,"[2] implying that he was some pleasure-seeking hellhound trying to destroy all that was holy in this world. In a torrential rain of rhetoric, Jerome condemned Jovinian's teachings as "vomit which he has thrown up."[3] With so much at stake, Bishops Ambrose of Milan and Augustine of Hippo couldn't help from entering the theological tussle. While Ambrose compared Jovinian to pack of hungry "wolves,"[4] Augustine called him a "monster," and attempted to counteract Jovinian's "poisons with all the power which the Lord gave me."[5]

Then came the death blow. Stripping Jovinian of spiritual protection and human dignity, the pope and emperor wielded their big sticks of church and state power. In the spring of 393, Pope Siricius convened a church council that promptly excommunicated not just Jovinian but several of his celibate-questioning cronies. In his letter of excommunication, the pope scorned Jovinian and friends as "the authors of a new heresy and blasphemy." The pope excoriated these men for "perverting the continence of the Old and New Testaments, interpreting it in a diabolical sense...[and forming] allies of their own insanity."[6] Last came a whip and a ship. An imperial edict ordered Jovinian to be "beaten with leaden whips" before being forced to sail away to a remote island off the coast of Dalmatia to suffer a life-long sentence of exile.[7]

DANGEROUS ENTERPRISE

Celibacy was sexy in early Christianity. Though hardly controversial today, Jovinian was entering a theological mine field when he suggested in the late fourth century that marriage was just as commendable as celibacy. Pope Siricius, far from allowing this monastic worm to get off the hook, was compelled to make an example out of him since he opposed Siricius's new plan for Christian clerics: life without sex. It was not enough for married clerics to have infrequent, and ideally, unpleasant sex with their lawfully wedded wives. Sex contaminated the sanctity of the church, and it had to be strictly regulated.

READING PAUL LIKE A RORSCHACH TEST

According to Peter Allen, "Sex was tied to everything [that]...Christians wanted to escape—the body, suffering, the endless cycle of birth and death. By turning away from sex, Christians could free the world from suffering and bring heaven closer to the here and now."[8] The apostle Paul agreed. Or, at least, many of his interpreters thought he did. Paul's teaching on sexuality, distilled in a mere forty verses in 1 Corinthians 7, was as influential as it was unclear. His words on this subject would go down as one of the great Rorschach tests of all times. Depending on one's context, inclination, and personal experiences, Paul would variously be interpreted as praising, tolerating, diminishing, or snubbing marriage. Unfortunately, not only is there scholarly disagreement about the precise historical context for Paul's reference to "the impending crisis" (1 Cor. 7:26), but there is no consensus when it comes to deciding exactly which statements came from Paul and which came from his followers and opponents.[9] Murkier still, we don't even know if Paul was a widower, whether his wife left him after he became a Christian, or whether he was a life-long celibate.

Whatever Paul intended in his renowned response to the Corinthians, the church fathers routinely interpreted him as urging celibacy but "suffering," after the manner of the King James Version, marriage. Fifth-century Bishop Theodoret of Cyrus represented many ancient Christians when he wrote that "Paul [was] praising chastity, condemning fornication and allowing conjugal relations."[10] Perhaps. But what many heard from Paul was what Theodoret's younger contemporary Bishop John Chrysostom heard when he put his ears to the railroad tracks of Paul's letter: "continence is better" than marriage.[11] And if continence was better, marriage was second-rate. If Chrysostom and many early Christians were correct, Paul would have been going against the grain of his Jewish upbringing. That's because marriage and procreation within Judaism were the highest callings of human existence. In a culture in which marriage and children was a divine blessing, celibacy and unfruitfulness was a curse. As one famous Jewish commentary on Genesis captured so poignantly:

> Man in celibacy is in sublime ignorance of what is meant by the words 'good,' 'help,' 'joy,' 'blessing,' 'peace,' and 'expiation of sin.' He is, in fact, not entitled to the dignified name of man.[12]

Although there were celebrated celibates in Jewish history, they were exceptions that made the rule—Judaism was a religion of the here and now, of the salt and the earth, of marriage and procreation.

CHRISTIAN ANARCHISTS

And that's exactly where many ancient Christians did not want to be. Throwing caution to the wind and their sex drives to the dust, countless Christians concluded that Christianity was primarily about a future bodiless existence in the kingdom of heaven. Though always in the minority, perhaps these radical Christians had a point. Didn't Jesus say, after all, that "at the resurrection people will neither marry nor be given in marriage [but] will be like the angels in heaven" (Matt. 22:30)? Didn't he also say that "there are those who choose to live [presently] like eunuchs for the sake of the kingdom of heaven" (Matt. 19:12)? If everyone was going to be celibate at the heavenly banquet, these radical men and women reasoned, why not prepare for

> The Augustan laws (of Emperor Augustus) rewarded families who had children and penalized men and women who did not get married. These laws promoted marriage and procreation for hundreds of years in the Roman Empire until Constantine, the first Christian emperor, overturned them. The family values of the earliest Christian society, in this way, were worlds apart from the family values of American conservatism.

the party while still on earth? Stated differently, recognizing that the heavenly tree of celibacy was good for food and pleasing to the eye, these Christians desired to eat this fruit earlier than anticipated.

Such Christian groups answered to many names: Gnostics, Phibionites, Manicheans, Marcionites, Montanists, Encratites, Valentinians. Although they did not celebrate their commonalities and would have instead regarded each other as suspicious at best or heretical at worst, what they shared was a deep distrust of human sexuality. Marcion, for instance, the infamous second-century believer whose Christian franchise had a monopoly on churches in the east, required complete celibacy from all baptized believers. His contemporary Tatian, a justly famous Christian from the Syriac-speaking world of the Middle East, did the same. For Tatian, the surest way to rise out of the deep pit of sin was to forever abandon one's sexual appetite. The cohort of Christians partial to this line of thinking in the east came to be known as the Encratites, or "self-controlled ones" in Greek. In the late fourth century, by which time Christianity had become respectable among the elite and the law of the land in the Roman Empire, the death penalty was the reward for any hapless souls that volunteered their association with this group. The reason behind such a stiff penalty was straightforward enough: A society without sex was no society at all. In a pure act of societal self-preservation, the Encratites were rooted out not as sexual prudes but as societal anarchists. Personal renunciation from sex was one thing, but corporate renunciation was communal suicide.

APOSTLES OF ABSTINENCE

It's not surprising that Gnostic Christians were casualties in the battle of orthodoxy. Their views on sex and reproduction sought to hasten the arrival of God's heavenly kingdom by depopulating life on earth. Before they exited the drama of early orthodox Christianity, however, they penned scores of so-called apocryphal New Testament documents. These Gnostic Christians, not unlike those of all ages, succumbed to the temptation of refashioning the earliest apostles in their own images. Here we encounter Jesus, the celibate twin of Thomas; Peter and Paul, the tenacious teachers of abstinence; and Philip, the adversary of the marriage bed. The highly sensational stories from the apocryphal Gospels were written in the second and third centuries for a Christian audience as curious as it was continent. Filling in the background of the stories of the Gospels and Acts in the New Testament, these Gnostic texts illustrate just how pervasive celibacy and virginity were becoming in the Christian world. They were the Christian antitypes of Danielle Steel and Nora Roberts.

As we briefly survey some of these apocryphal Christian stories, we step back into a culture that often equated salvation with cessation of sex. In the *Acts of the Apostles Peter and Paul*, for instance, the two holy apostles were arrested not for preaching repentance but for urging two high-born female converts to cease having sex with their powerful husbands, who happened to be the emperor and the prefect of Rome. Not surprisingly, they were swiftly killed—Paul by beheading since he was a Roman citizen and Peter by crucifixion upside-down. In the beloved *Acts of Paul and Thecla*, Paul was likewise persecuted for teaching sexual abstinence. Rather than encouraging modest sex within marriage, the apostle exclaimed instead—in a sort of celibate homage to Jesus's Beatitudes from the Sermon on the Mount: "Blessed are they that have kept the flesh chaste," "blessed are they that have wives as not having them," and "blessed are the bodies of the virgins."[13] To which many at the time affirmed a hearty "Amen." Naturally, though, this teaching had to be stopped. Though providentially escaping death, Paul was nonetheless flogged in this story for "depriv[ing] young men of wives, and maidens of husbands."[14] In a similar way, Thecla was rejected by her mother and others in the community for renouncing sin for Christ. In short, as the holy apostles learned the hard way, it was a serious crime in the ancient world to deprive a society of its livelihood: offspring.

But Peter and Paul weren't the only apostles preaching the good news of celibacy in these texts. There were plenty of apocryphal Christian books showing other apostles doing the same, three of which are worthy of comment. In the *Acts of Philip*, both Philip and Bartholomew were tortured for teaching abstinence within marriage—inciting the ire of the pagan proconsul, a man "raging like an unbroken horse" after his wife threatened that he would have to "prepare [himself] to live in chastity" from thence forward.[15] This stallion would not be without his mare. Elsewhere, in the *Acts and Martyrdom of Saint Matthew the Apostle*, Jesus told Matthew, "I am…the crown of the virgins…the self-control of the once married…[and] the boast of the widowed," urging Matthew to teach celibacy as a matter of principle.[16] Finally, in the *Acts of the Holy Apostle Thomas*, both Thomas and his twin brother Jesus Christ urged a newly married couple to never consummate their marriage in order to keep themselves pure from the "filthy lust" of sexual intercourse.[17] Combined, these apocryphal gospels, by no means unique in the library of early Christian Gnosticism, attempted to "encourage Christian believers to live a life of celibacy or, if they [were] married, to refrain from sexual intercourse so as to better serve Christ."[18]

IN THE LINE OF SEXUAL SELF-DENIAL

But it wasn't just fringe Christians who cautioned against sex. It did not take long before there was a well-manicured movement of celibate men and women growing in both the Christian East and the West, which would bloom in the centuries to come. Writing in the second century, Tertullian directed an entire book to the common practice of virgins being "veiled" in church services. (Here it's important to note that "to veil" in Latin, nubire [hence "nuptials" in English], meant "to marry.") During this ritual, bishops effectively married women to a life of virginity by presenting them with a veil that they would wear in church as a sign of their marriage to the heavenly bridegroom. Partitioned off in churches from the mere mortals who engaged in sexual intercourse, these virgins were not brides of Christ, they were living angels. Although more mainstream groups paid lip-service to the respectability of marriage, inwardly—and frequently outwardly—they regarded it as second-rate Christianity. After all, if the body belonged fully to the Lord, as Paul consistently taught, what right did temporary tenants have to rent it out for the sake of lust? And if Christians were "slaves" of Christ, a potent metaphor in Roman society that is muted on modern North American ears, then these "slaves" were required to use their bodies in whatever manner their master required. And increasingly in the ancient world, Christians believed their master required his slaves to be continent.

The fourth century was the turning point of clerical celibacy. Historian David Hunter argues that "[Pope] Siricius's letter [against Jovinian in the 390s] marked the first time in the history of Christianity that the superiority of celibacy over marriage was officially defined as doctrine, and conversely, that its denial was labeled as 'heresy.'"[19] Though encountering resistance among married clergy who wanted to keep one foot in the church and the other in the bedroom, Siricius sternly opposed clerical sex and legislated against those who broke their vows of virginity.

> Just as *nubire* ("to cover with a veil") was the Latin word used of women when getting married, so *ducere* ("to lead") was the word used of men. In this way, a woman "veiled herself" while a man "led," in the sense that he led the woman back to his father's house.

Likening Christian clerics to Old Testament priests and Levites who abstained from sex before overseeing sacrifices, Siricius reasoned that the church's sacraments could best be safeguarded by clerics who had refrained from the ritual contaminant of sex. His reasoning on this matter was straightforward enough:

> Why were the priests [in the old dispensation] bidden to take up their dwelling in the temple, far from their homes [and thus their marriage beds], during their year of service? Why but for the purpose that they might have no carnal intercourse even with their wives but in the radiance of an upright conscience offer an acceptable gift unto God.[20]

Siricius believed that priestly rituals such as the administration of Communion were contaminated by sexually active clerics. There was something about sex and the sacred that didn't play well together. But it wasn't just that. Pope Siricius likewise concluded that only sex-free priests had the street credibility needed to take charge of the growing number of celibate men and women in their dioceses.[21] Although the book of Hebrews teaches that the celibate Jesus was able "to empathize with our weaknesses" (4:15), married priests were increasingly unable to gain the respect of the spiritually continent.

CHAMPION OF CELIBACY

Many of Siricius's contemporaries thought similarly. Jerome, who had retreated to the Holy Land in order to tame the darkened forest of his loins, was one of the most prominent champions of celibacy in the early church. His reasons for commending celibacy were not identical with Siricius's,[22] but his praise of celibacy was matched only by his disdain of marriage. For Jerome, the sole benefit of marriage was that it had the potential of producing more virgins. When it came to deciding between the Old Testament dictum "it is not good for the man to be alone" (Gen. 2:18) and the New Testament saying "it is best not to touch a woman" (1 Cor. 7:1), he chose the latter. In comparison to marriage, he likened virginity to the "rose [in] the thorns, the gold [in] the earth, the pearl [in] the shell."[23] Once virginity was extracted from the shell of marriage, the shell could be happily trod under foot. According to Jerome, "virginity [was] fine corn, wedlock [was] barley, and fornication [was]

***The Temptation of St. Jerome* by Francisco de Zurbarán.**

cow-dung."[24] In his hierarchy of humanity, virgins were naturally at the top. They were angels perching high in the heavens, while at the bottom were sin-streaked mortals—bits of barley and dung that couldn't keep themselves from doing the deed. Sacrificing their sexual desires on the altar of godliness, "Christ love[d] virgins more than others."[25]

Jerome's prescription for virgins was a bitter pill to swallow. Because women were by nature weak and vulnerable, he reasoned, they were never to even "look upon a man, especially a young man,"[26] for fear that the mere appearance of a male would ignite lust that would consummate in fornication. It was best, he recommended, for a sex-free woman to stay inside the house, to spend day and night in prayer and fasting, to read the Bible, to wear coarse clothing, to refrain from sweets and alcohol, and to take lots of cold showers, if any at all. Women were to set their gaze on the Virgin Mary as the paragon of perfection. Eve, by contrast, provided a potent counter-model. Though "in paradise Eve was a virgin," she prostituted herself to sex after the devil seduced her.[27] After locating ground zero of humanity's weakness, the devil had been readying, aiming, and firing his temptations at men's loins and women's navels ever since. The best way to protect oneself from the devil's schemes was "to have as little traffic as possible" with the opposite sex, and then in a public place with as much space between genders as would not stimulate excitement.[28]

"For Jerome," explains one commentator, "sex and procreation were irrevocably associated with sin and punishment."[29] Thus sex and reproduction were activities best avoided. Without at all putting Jerome's theology on the couch of Freudian psychoanalysis, it's likely that his personal encounter with sex as a country boy newly enraptured by city life in Rome tainted his view of human sexuality. According to his biographer J. N. D. Kelly, "Jerome's student days were marked by sexual adventures to which he was afterwards to look back with loathing." Kelly makes the case that Jerome "was strongly sexed," and that his desire to be free from sexual captivity was what drove him into the desert and away from the sexual temptations of city life.[30] He was a man haunted by his sexual history living in an age when salvation and celibacy were as linked as peanut butter and jelly.

THE AUGUSTINE RULE

Many scholars think the same is true for Augustine, one of the most influential theologians in the history of Western Christianity. Well before he took up the title of "Doctor of the Church," let alone bishop of a rural North African diocese, he had to overcome his addiction to sex. More than fifteen hundred years before Billy Graham vowed to never eat, meet, or travel alone with a woman not related to him in order to avoid any appearance of sexual malfeasance, Augustine had been denying even female relatives access to his bishop's palace unaccompanied.[31] Augustine, after all, was a man with a past. He was a self-confessed slave to sexual sin who literally wrote the book on sexual impropriety. As he penned in his famous autobiography *Confessions*:

> From [my] perverse will came lust, and slavery to lust became a habit, and the habit, being constantly yielded to, became a necessity. These were like links, hanging each to each (which is why I call it a chain), and they held me fast in a hard slavery.[32]

At the tender age of sixteen, Augustine fastened the first chain of lust around his neck by taking up residence with his girlfriend. During this union he indulged in thirteen years of unrestrained appetite. Because he was of a higher social standing—and, quite frankly, because he was ambitious—Augustine terminated his affair after his mother arranged for a bride that would make him publicly respectable. This was despite the fact that he had fathered a son with this unnamed object of sexual gratification and that she would now be deprived of her lover and son (since Roman law gave children to fathers upon annulments). However, because his future bride was not of age, Augustine's sexual addiction compelled him to redirect his torrent of lust toward an older woman as a sort of "stopgap mistress."[33]

But then something unexpected happened. Thanks to his mother's prayers and his bishop's teaching, the incomparable Ambrose of Milan, Augustine got religion. As a man of his time, Augustine believed that the cool waters of baptism were the surest salve of the hot desires of youth. Moving away from his second girlfriend and canceling his wedding plans, he concluded that union with Christ signified separation from sex. As he later wrote in his book *Soliloquies*, "I have decided that there is nothing I should avoid so much as marriage. I know nothing which brings the manly mind down from the heights more than a woman's caresses."[34]

After stepping into the baptismal waters of Milan in 386 and thereby, according to the standard doctrine of Catholicism, obtaining salvation and returning to a state of Garden of Eden-like purity, all the previous sexual sins of Augustine were wiped away like the eraser of a filthy blackboard. In many ways, as historian Margaret Miles suggests, "Augustine's conversion was…a release from the compulsive pursuit of sex."[35] Indeed, salvation for Augustine was not just freedom from sin—it was freedom from sex. As he admitted to God, "you [and you alone] freed me from the bondage of my desire for sex."[36]

Still, the reminiscences of those warm—yet sin laden—caresses of his former lovers, remained firmly lodged in his overactive imagination. Augustine bravely laid bare how he was haunted by sexual fantasies and debauched by nocturnal emissions even years after becoming a celibate Christian:

> But there still live images of the things which my habit has fixed there. These images come into my thoughts, and, though when I am awake they are strengthless, in sleep they not only cause pleasure but go so far as to obtain assent and something very like reality. These images, though real, have such an effect on my soul, in my flesh, that false visions in my sleep obtain from me what true visions cannot when I am awake…Almighty God, surely your hand is powerful enough to cure all the sicknesses of my soul and…to quench even the lustful impulses of my sleep…so that my soul, disentangled from the birdlime of concupiscence, may follow me to you; so that it may not be in revolt against itself and may not, even in dreams, succumb to or even give the slightest assent to those degrading corruptions which by means of sensual images actually disturb and pollute the flesh.[37]

Although Augustine took a higher road than his acquaintance Jerome when it came to discussing marriage, he was hardly the enthusiast of an institution that was consummated in concupiscence. As he bluntly stated, "the genital organs have become…the private property of lust,"[38] leading readers to wonder what good could come from organs under the possession of a demonic desire. Marriage in itself was not a sin, he consistently claimed, but sexual intercourse among married couples was tainted by the flesh. Sex was to be performed out of deference to the "weaker spouse," he conceded, but always "for the sake of having children."[39] This was Augustine's two-edged sword. Though allowing sex within marriage for the sake of procreation, he nevertheless maintained that there was no justification for married couples to replenish

Conversion of Saint Augustine **by Fra Angelico.**

Concupiscence is a theological term in the Latin West referring to an inordinate sexual desire. It is both a sin and a punishment for the original sin of Adam and Eve, transmitted from generation to generation.

the population—even when they produced Christian children! Commenting on Genesis's command to "be fruitful and multiply" (Gen. 1:28), Augustine was convinced that this was solely applicable to Old Testament saints. He argued that there were presently too many people living in the world, so those "who desire to marry solely for the sake of having children should be advised to avail themselves rather of the greater benefit of abstinence."[40] He even admitted in a sermon that the sexual drive was so strong that couples could not—and would not—abstain from sex, but they would be forgiven by saying the Lord's Prayer as penance.[41]

Augustine's teaching on sex was a theological Rubik's Cube. Though suggesting ease of understanding, it was virtually impossible for anyone to put all the color schemes in order. Augustine clearly understood that Scripture affirmed marriage, and he even eloquently elaborated on the three "goods" of marriage in one of his treaties, but he also believed that Adam and Eve's sin forever tarnished sexual intercourse. He famously taught that all children came immediately "under the power of the Devil" upon conception since they were generated through lust,[42] leading his contemporary Christian opponents to argue that Augustine suggested that marriage was the invention of the Devil and that sex between couples was "murder" since men and women could only pass on their spiritual evil and none of their spiritual good.[43] It was a serious accusation that subsequent generations of Christians would have to decide for themselves.

STAYING A MAN, BECOMING A MAN

But that wasn't all of the legacy Augustine left. According to the august bishop, nothing brings down the "manly mind [*animus virile*]" like "a woman's caresses."[44] Though unpleasant to modern readers, the early Christian emphasis on virginity and celibacy was an emphasis on what Latin speakers called *virtus*. This is the source of the English word "virtue," though the Latin is best translated as "manliness," "manhood," or "virility," as can be seen in the Latin term for "man"—*vir*. According to ancient medical literature, *virtus* was about preserving one's semen. As a second-century physician explained, frequent ejaculation made one "torpid, relaxed, spiritless, timid, stupid, enfeebled, shriveled, inactive, pale, whitish, [and] effeminate."[45] The loss of too much semen, in other words, made a man a woman. Worse yet, suggested the Christian theologian Tertullian, the loss of too much semen made a man a soulless corpse. As he reasoned in his book *On the Soul*, "I speak of this at the risk of seeming improper, but…do we not feel something of our very soul [*anima*] go out from us [when ejaculating]"?[46] All things the same, he and others concluded, it was best to keep one's *virtus*—and *anima*—intact by preserving one's seed.

The same cannot be said about a woman. For many male Christians, women were hardly "the better half" of the world's population. Instead, women were merely incomplete—and thus imperfect—men. Whereas males were primarily spiritual by nature, females were regarded as carnal. The frequent male urging for women to embrace a life of virginity was an invitation to transcend one's gender—in short, it was an invitation to become a man. As Jerome wrote to a widow named Demetrias, "as long as a woman [longs] for birth and children, she is as different from man as body is from soul. But when she wishes to serve Christ more than the world [by becoming a virgin], she will cease to be a woman and *will be called man*."[47]

This is strange stuff. It's like a backhanded slap to our faces. Ancient Christians, much to our dislike, sank sin deep into the sexual organs of humanity. It was a common belief that sex was the result of the fall of Adam and Eve from Paradise. Before the fall, many Christians believed that Adam and Eve existed in some sort of ethereal wonderland devoid of female lust and male libido. But afterward sexual desire, what was commonly called concupiscence, swelled up in the loins and navels of humanity's forbearers. Adam and Eve's bodily union consummated their corporate fall into the pit of sexual depravity. Under this distressing interpretation, "the libido," mused Christian bishop Caesarius of Arles, was "a

Fourth-century Mosaic of Women Exercising in Villa Romana del Casale, Sicily. Courtesy of Kenton Greening.

punishment for sin, a consequence of the Fall from Grace, and the root of all evil."[48] Bishop Gregory of Nyssa was even more candid: "Bodily procreation…is the origin not of life but of death."[49] The solution to humanity's sin problem was not just salvation; it was also celibacy. By turning away from sex, virgins recaptured life before sin. They recreated the Garden of Eden. As Ambrose of Milan explained to virgins like his darling sister, "You are paradise."[50] By refusing sexual intercourse, they were literally saving human civilization.

THE VIRGINS, THE CELIBATES, AND THE CHASTE

Ancient Christians have left a sexual legacy that many moderns would like to forget. It's hardly worth denying that early Christians disparaged the female body and regarded it as some sort of portal to the dark side. They made sex shameful, prompting many Western Christians to associate sexuality with sin and guilt. They also bequeathed a sexual caste system to posterity that stripped marriage of its dignity. There were the virgins, the celibate, and, alas, the chaste. At the top of this caste system were the virgins. These were the men and, especially, women whose sacred and sex-free lives on earth anticipated life in heaven. They were the "holy ones" who could intercede to God for their sexually tainted communities like a priest atoned for the sins of his flock. Next were the celibates or the continents. These were the men and women who had once tasted of the forbidden fruit but were now prepared to discard the half-eaten apple in exchange for a life free from the sinful pleasures of sex. Such men and women were often widows and widowers, but it was also common for married couples to refrain from doing the deed as a way to curry God's favor in the life thereafter.

> "At one point in the Gospel of the Egyptians Salome asks Jesus, 'How long will death prevail?' That is to say, how long will this miserable material world and all its finitudes last? Jesus gives a terse response: 'For as long as you women bear children.' Once there are no more bodies being produced, there will be no more prisons for the divine sparks to inhabit, and death will, obviously, be no more. Salome then responds, 'Then I have done well not to bear children.' Jesus affirms her choice, saying, 'Eat every herb, but not the one that is bitter.' In other words, it is best to avoid the painful life experience of giving birth."[53]

Finally, there were the chaste. These were Christian couples too weak to "manage their own vessels" (1 Thess. 4:4). As Jerome so painfully made clear, these were the ones that Christ loved least. Their intercourse with each other was to be dutifully regulated. Such married couples, an ancient author advised, "should consider sexual pleasures justified *only...when accomplished for the purpose of procreation of children*...But mere pleasure hunting is unjust and unlawful, even if it is within marriage."[51] As Christianity institutionalized, pleasure hunting would be gunned down with gusto. A casual glance through medieval Christian law codes makes one wonder whether couples had any sex at all. Not just was sex prohibited during penance, on Sundays, during Lent and during many other sacred days throughout the liturgical calendar, but sex was *Verboten* when a woman was menstruating, pregnant, or nursing, and there was a list as detailed as the *Kama Sutra* when it came to sexual postures and practices that were off-limits to lawfully married couples. So shameful had sex become that one fifth-century church statute cautioned newly married couples from having intercourse on their wedding nights so that they wouldn't invalidate the nuptial blessing they received at the service. Around the same time period, Saint Caesarius of Arles forbade newly married couples from entering a church within thirty days of their wedding so as not to pollute the temple of God with the impurity of sex.[52] Living in an age today when many consider marriage the heart of the gospel, early Christians were too happy to dissolve that union altogether, or at least strictly regulate it, for the good of society and for the good of a person's soul.

ENDNOTES

1 David Hunter, *Marriage, Celibacy, and Heresy in Ancient Christianity: The Jovinianist Controversy* (Oxford: Oxford University Press, 2007), 1.

2 David Hunter, "General Introduction," in *The Works of Saint Augustine: A Translation for the 21st Century*, vol. 9, *Marriage and Virginity*, trans. Ray Kearney (Hyde Park, NY: New City Press, 1999), 15.

3 Quoted in J. N. D. Kelly, *Jerome: His Life, Writings, and Controversies* (New York: Harper & Row, 1975), 186.

4 Quoted in Hunter, *Marriage, Celibacy, and Heresy in Ancient Christianity*, 1.

5 Quoted in Hunter, "General Introduction," 9:15.

6 Dale Martin, *Sex and Single Savior: Gender and Sexuality in Biblical Interpretation* (Louisville, KY: Westminster John Knox Press, 2006), 117.

7 Quoted in Hunter, *Marriage, Celibacy, and Heresy in Ancient Christianity*, 243.

8 Peter Allen, *The Wages of Sin: Sex and Disease, Pasts and Present* (Chicago: University of Chicago Press, 2000), 5.

9 For as good a reconstruction as any, see Richard Hays, *First Corinthians*, Interpretation: A Bible Commentary for Teaching and Preaching (Louisville, KY: Westminster John Knox Press, 2011), 110–129.

10 Theodoret of Cyr, "Commentary on the First Epistle to the Corinthians 22," in *1-2 Corinthians*, Ancient Christian Commentary on Scripture, vol. VIII, ed. Gerald Bray (Downers Grove, IL: InterVarsity Press, 1999), 59.

11 Chrysostom, "Homilies on the Epistles of Paul to the Corinthians 19.3," in *1-2 Corinthians*, 62.

12 "Genesis Rabbah," in Charles Francis Home, *The Sacred Books and Early Literature of the East* (New York: Parke, Austin, and Lipscomb, 1917), 52.

13 Quoted in Annemarie Kidder, *Women, Celibacy, and the Church: Towards a Theology of the Single Life* (New York: The Crosswood Publishing Company, 2003), 150.

14 Ibid., 66.

15 Ibid., 71.

16 Ibid., 79.

17 Ibid., 83

18 Ibid., 100.

19 David Hunter, "Asceticism and Clerical Authority in Late Ancient Christianity," in *The Cultural Turn in Late Ancient Studies: Gender, Asceticism, and Historiography*, ed. Dale Martin and Patricia Miller (Durham, NC: Duke University Press, 2005), 119.

20 Quoted in Hunter, *Marriage, Celibacy, and Heresy in Ancient Christianity*, 215.

21 Kidder, *Women, Celibacy, and the Church*, 162.

22 According to Hunter, Siricius "focused on strengthening the structures of the clerical office," while Jerome opposed Jovinian and clerical sex in order "to foster ascetic practice," *Marriage, Celibacy, and Heresy in Ancient Christianity*, 241.

23 Jerome, Letter 22.20.

24 Jerome, "Letter 48," in *Nicene and Post-Nicene Fathers*, vol. 6, *Jerome: Letters and Select Works*, ed. Philip Schaff and Henry Wallace (New York: Cosimo, 2007), 74.

25 Jerome, *Against Jovinian* 12, quoted in Evans, *Sin and Salvation*, 117.

26 Jerome, *To Demetrias,* 12.

27 Jerome, *Letter* 22.19.

28 James Brundage, *Law, Sex, and Christian Society in Medieval Europe* (Chicago: University of Chicago Press, 1987), 101.

29 Hunter, *Marriage, Celibacy, and Heresy in Ancient Christianity*, 227.

30 Kelly, *Jerome*, 21.

31 Brown, *The Body and Society*, 396.

32 Augustine, "Confessions 8.5," in *The Confessions of Saint Augustine*, trans. Rex Warner (New York: Signet Classic, 2001), 158.

33 Brown, *The Body and Society*, 392.

34 Quoted in Hunter, "General Introduction," in *The Works of Saint Augustine*, 9:10.

35 Margaret Miles, *Desire and Delight: A New Reading of Augustine's Confessions* (Eugene, OR: Wipf & Stock, 2006; original 1991), 33.

36 Augustine, "Confessions 8.6," 160.

37 Augustine, "Confessions 10.30," 231.

38 Augustine, "City of God 14.19," in *St Augustine: City of God*, trans. Henry Bettenson (London: Penguin Group, 1984), 581.

39 Augustine, "Confessions 4.2," 57.

40 Augustine, "The Excellence of Marriage 9.9," in *The Works of Augustine*, 9:41.

41 See *Sermons: Part III-Sermons (341-400)*, vol. 10, *The Works of Augustine: A Translation for the 21st Century*, trans. Edmund Hill (Hyde Park, NY: New City Press, 1999), 164.

42 Augustine, "4.4," quoted in Elizabeth Clark, *St. Augustine on Marriage and Celibacy*, ed. Elizabeth Clark (Washington, DC: The Catholic University of America, 1996), 91.

43 Clark, St. *Augustine on Marriage and Celibacy*, 86.

44 *Patrologia Latina*, vol. 32, ed. J. –P Migne (Paris, 1841), 878.

45 Peter Allen, *The Wages of Sin*, 83.

46 Tertullian, "On the Soul 27.5," quoted in Brown, *The Body and Society*, 17.

47 Jerome, Commentary on the Epistle to Ephesus 2, quoted in Evans, Sex and Salvation, 69.

48 Brundage, *Law, Sex, and Christian Society in Medieval Europe*, 84.

49 Teresa Shaw, "Sex and Sexual Renunciation," in *The Early Christian World*, vol. 1, ed. Philip Esler (London and New York: Routledge, 2000), 416.

50 Quoted in Hunter, *Marriage, Celibacy, and Heresy in Ancient Christianity*, 227.

51 Quoted in Teresa Shaw, "Sex and Sexual Renunciation," in *The Early Christian World*, vol. 1, ed. Philip Esler (London and New York: Routledge, 200), 409; see also Musonius Rufus, "Concerning Sexual Pleasure," in *Greek and Roman Sexualities: A Sourcebook*, ed. Jennifer Larson (London and New York: Bloomsbury Academic, 2012), 175.

52 Brundage, *Law, Sex, and Christian Society in Medieval Europe*, 91.

53 Bart Ehrman, *Peter, Paul, and Mary Magdalene: The Followers of Jesus in History and Legend* (Oxford: Oxford University Press, 2006), 233.

Chapter 10

CONVERTING THE NATIONS—MISSION AND SOCIETY

Residents of the ancient city were hastily filling the beautifully decorated rooms of the church with dirt, rubble, and who knows what else. In between desperate moments of packing mud with their hands and wiping sweat from their foreheads, some of the dazed people must have gazed at the colorful biblical artwork adorning the building's walls and wondered what in the world it might mean. *Who is that man walking on the water? Who is that woman at the well talking to? Why is that man carrying a mat?* It was probably the first time many of these people had ever stepped foot in a church building—and if it wasn't, it certainly was their last. Whatever curious thoughts may have arisen in their frightened heads that day, we will never know. The residents of this Syrian fortress quickly left the church and proceeded to fill up the other religious buildings with mud and debris, including the cult dedicated to the god Mithras as well as a newly restored Jewish synagogue.

Philosophers today tell us that perspective is everything. We can't help but agree. While brigades of civilians passed dirt in clay jars from person to person under the supervision of Roman soldiers in Dura-Europos in the year 256, they were preparing for the end of the world. They were right to do so. This was their doomsday. This was their final stand. Most everyone in the city, Christian and pagan alike, died. The few who didn't were sold into slavery, vanishing from the pages of history like a grain of sand in the Arabian Desert. Although the Persians conquered the city that day, no one ever rebuilt Dura-Europos. This once-thriving city sitting at the crossroads of the ancient world became a veritable ghost town until archaeologists in the 1920s and 1930s began unearthing artifacts and interpreting their finds. To their great delight, last-minute attempts to fortify the city wall by residents in the third century preserved many structures. Among the structures preserved, archaeologists discovered an elaborately decorated and recently renovated church—perhaps the oldest church known to exist in the world. Early Christians, far from being confined to the Roman Empire, had been converted well beyond the Mediterranean basin, and they were not about to be halted now—not even by the likes of chemical warfare.

THE WORLD THEIR PARISH

We know more about the end of Christianity in Dura-Europos than the beginning. Fortunately, that's not always the case. While Christianity in the Roman Empire developed in fits and starts, with a growth rate at less than four percent annually during the first several centuries,[1] it flourished in many other regions. According to the book of Acts, the earliest Jewish Christians in Jerusalem had traveled "as far as Phoenicia and Cyprus and Antioch" (11:19–26), where they made many Jewish converts before turning to Gentile Greeks. The book of Acts also states that it was in Antioch—not in Rome or Athens or even in Jerusalem—where the term *Christian* was coined.[2] Antioch was a fitting location for Christianity's emergence, for it was a cosmopolitan city with an enchantingly diverse ethnic population. Not only was this metropolis the launching pad of Paul's missionary journeys to the Gentiles, but it was also the place of Peter's earliest ministry to the Jews. Indeed, as a faith forever destined to become more than a mere Roman religion, the early Christians interpreted Antioch as just the beginning. To paraphrase John Wesley, the world was their parish, and they were not about to forfeit their rights. Didn't Jesus himself command his followers to go out and make disciples of *all the nations*?

NOT ENOUGH JAM TO COVER THE TOAST

According to early memory, that's exactly what Jesus's followers did. They traveled far and wide, high and low, down and dirty for the sake of the gospel, converting scores of hell-bound pagans and spellbinding them with miraculous signs and deeds of wonder. Andrew converted the Greeks, Matthew the Ethiopians, Bartholomew the Indians, Thomas the Afghanis, Jude the Armenians, Simon the Britains, and Judas Thaddeus the Iranians. These globetrotting gospel-heralds conquered wild beasts, outwitted pagan philosophers, raised the dead, healed the sick, and wrestled with demons. If these are stories too good to be true, that's because they probably never happened. Not at least in the exact way the stories have been recorded. In a world where lineage was ev-

Christ Walking on Water.
Photograph courtesy of Marsyas.

erything, and truth was often stranger than fiction, even the most provincial of church traditions was compelled to trace its heritage to one of the disciples of Christ. With little exaggeration, there were twenty churches claiming the relics of every one disciple. The only problem, of course, was that there were only so many disciples to go around, and they probably didn't live long enough, travel wide enough, or have enough body parts to have founded as many churches as laid claim. The legends of their lives are probably just that—wonderfully exotic, if not naughty, tales attempting to fill in the juicy details of their lives that are incapable of being authenticated.

JESUS'S TWIN BROTHER PREACHES CELIBACY IN INDIA

The most romantic tale in ancient Christianity is that the apostle Thomas sailed to India and converted the Hindu people to Christianity before the apostles Peter and Paul had even stepped foot in Rome. This has been a stubbornly persistent claim. According to the apocryphal *Acts of Thomas*, written around the year 200 from Syria, the apostle Thomas was commissioned by Jesus to convert India under the guise of being a skillful carpenter capable of building a magnificent palace fit for a king. Like an apple not falling far from the tree, Thomas had learned the family business of carpentry from his famous father, Joseph. Shockingly perhaps, Thomas was apprenticed while working side-by-side with his twin brother, Jesus of Nazareth. That's right—according to the opening lines of the *Acts of Thomas*, Thomas, which means "twin" in Aramaic (just as *Didymus* means this in Greek), was the identical twin of Jesus Christ. After living a lifetime under the shadow of his doppelganger, Judas Thomas was willing to travel the world over to tell of the glories of his brother's harrowing death, victorious resurrection, and mastery of continence.

> There are two competing Thomas traditions in India today. One group, called Northists, claims origins from the time of the apostle Thomas. Another group, called Southists, claim a fourth-century genesis through the likes of a Christian merchant named Thomas of Cana, who immigrated with 72 Christian families and several clergymen to southern India in the 340s.

Here's how the story goes. After Jesus had died and been resurrected, the remaining apostles were tasked with casting lots to see which apostle would have the responsibility of preaching in each region of the known world. Judas Thomas, ever the doubter, could hardly believe it when he drew a lot for the region of India—about as far from ancient Jerusalem as Timbuktu is from Tallahassee. If it weren't for the special appearance of Jesus, who confirmed that Thomas was to sail to India to convert the king as a slave, Thomas would have drifted off into the night and regarded the whole situation as a dream gone awry. Arriving in India as an undercover missionary, Judas Thomas's first act of evangelism was to attend a banquet celebrating the marriage of King Gundaphar's only daughter. It would be the perfect place to preach his version of the gospel, which, as we have seen in the previous chapter, centered on celibacy.

Thomas distinguished himself almost at once by his prudish behavior and dour disposition. As a flute girl danced provocatively in front of him at the marriage banquet, the sexually chaste Thomas lowered his gaze and "was looking all the time on the ground." To counteract the sexual allure of the flute girl, Thomas sang a Christian ditty lauding the sexual purity of the bride of Christ, the church. The king, impressed by Thomas's sexual scruples, requested that he pray for his daughter in—of all places—the "bridal chamber" itself. He shouldn't have. Rather than requesting the Lord for a fruitful marriage overgrown with generations of child-bearing descendants, Thomas prayed to his brother and God that this young married couple would receive "whatever you know to be beneficial for them," which, surprise-surprise, turned out to be the gift of celibacy.

> As we have seen in another chapter, there is an entire Thomas tradition in the early church claiming that Judas Thomas was the twin brother of Jesus of Nazareth. This is seen most clearly in the *Acts of Thomas* and *Gospel of Thomas*, both written in the 100s.

When Thomas left the bridal chamber after offering this most unusual prayer, his twin brother Jesus appeared in his place as if by magic. Like worried parents warning their kids about the dangers of sexual intercourse on their way to a high school prom, Thomas's twin brother lectured the honeymooners from the marriage bed while they set on separate chairs. "Remember," Jesus explained to them, "what my brother [Thomas] spoke with you, and know to whom he committed you; and know that as soon as you preserve yourselves from this filthy intercourse, you become pure temples, and are saved." Returning to their daughter's bedroom the following morning, the king and queen were anxious to learn about the fireworks that must have discharged during the wedding night. They were sorely disappointed. Like an aged married couple now reposing in separate beds, the newlyweds were sleeping in different parts of the room. To the chagrin of the parents, the young married couple never consummated their marriage out of the conviction that they were now married "to the true Husband," Christ. Enraged, the king ordered the capture of "that sorcerer," Judas Thomas, so that he could put him to death for attempting the greatest act of sabotage in the ancient world: putting an end to the royal line and starving a kingdom of kingship.[3]

Despite the amusing yet historically unlikely suggestion that Jesus had a twin brother and that he and this twin, Judas Thomas, worked as sidekicks to save the second-largest country in the world from the sin of sexual intercourse, many scholars have slowly warmed to the possibility that this story may have a kernel of truth. The noted historian of Christianity in Asia, Samuel Moffett, by no means an academic wet behind the ears, has compellingly argued that underneath the Thomas tradition in India "lies a foundation of fact."[4] He may very well be right.

> "India and all its countries, and those bordering on it even to the farthest sea, received the Apostle's Hand of Priesthood from Judas Thomas, who was Guide and Ruler in the church he built there."[17]

The legendary accretions of the story notwithstanding, there's archaeological evidence that a certain Gundaphar reigned in India during the same time Thomas is reputed to have ministered there, and there's no doubt that trade and travel between the Roman and Indian Empires thrived in the first century of our Lord. There's also the inconvertible testimony of an ancient and enduring community of Christians in India, who have lived in this region of the world for who knows how long—but cer-

Tomb of St. Thomas the Apostle in Mylapore, India. Courtesy of Mathen Payyappilly Palakkappilly.

tainly more than a millennium. This Christian community has preserved the tomb of the apostle Thomas for centuries under the conviction that he died there as a martyr to the faith. We even have reports from Emperor Valens in the late fourth century attempting to discourage Christians from worshiping at the shrine there erected to Thomas.

Finally, there's the many literary references attesting to Thomas's ministry in India, confirmed by various Christian authors and documents originating during the third and fourth centuries. In addition to the *Acts of Thomas* and the third-century *Didascalia Apostolorum*, such a literary list includes a veritable Who's Who of Early Christian Churchmen: Gregory of Nazianzus, Ambrose of Milan, Jerome, Paulinus of Nola, Ephrem the Syrian, and Gregory of Tours. Either every one of these church fathers was mistakenly using the same source book, or they had put their fingers on an interesting tradition rooted in fact.

PYRAMIDAL CHRISTIANITY

If the story of Thomas's conversion of the king of India to Christianity is true, it would have been slightly unusual since the king's subjects didn't convert along with him. It wasn't the Protestant reformers, after all, who invented the notion of *cuius regio, eius religio*—"whose region, his religion." Religion and state had always been a package deal. It was the modern equivalent of death and taxes. Typically, *religio* followed the *rex* of a particular *regio*, meaning that the "religion" of the "king" was that of the "region." Indeed, a common, but by no means exclusive, formula for Christian expansion in the ancient world was the amassing of converts in a top-down fashion. What we might call pyramidal Christianity, the strategy was as follows: Convert the royals to Christianity and everyone else will fall into place. Of course, this style of conversion was never as sanitized as we might imagine, and there were plenty of exceptions, yet it was the manner in which many non-Roman nation states came to adopt Christianity as their state religion, including Armenia, Georgia, and Ethiopia. After the royals were converted, then followed the aristocracy, the military, and finally the plebeians and peasants.

THE OLDEST CHRISTIAN NATION ON EARTH

Despite its obscurity today in the Western world, Armenia's religious heritage rivals that of any nation. According to a much-cherished tradition, Armenia is the mother of all humanity. And a mother on two separate occasions, no less. The Garden of Eden—where life was born—as well as Noah's ark—where all of life was preserved—were reportedly located within Armenia's blessed borders.[5] Given such a lush biblical history, it's not surprising that Armenia lays claim to the title of the oldest continuous Christian nation in existence. Even today, this mountainous Western Asian nation boasts one of the highest percentages of Christians anywhere in the world, surpassing the percentage of Christians in the United States by an impressive twenty percent.[6]

Christ and the Twelve Apostles. Courtesy of Dnalor 01.

We scholars, of course, are reluctant to bestow such esteemed titles for fear of error or oversight, but the early church historian Sozomen had no such scruples. Relying on the best scholarship available, Sozomen reported that "the Armenians were the first to embrace Christianity."[7] Armenians agree. With unbridled enthusiasm, they have argued for centuries that their country was the first in the world to adopt Christianity as its state religion—a dozen years before Emperor Constantine even converted to Christianity, let alone decades before his successors made Christianity the official religion of the empire. Perhaps despite, or because of, its great Christian heritage, Armenia has also historically been one of the most persecuted countries in the world, leading historian Aziz Atiya to record that Armenia's Christian saints and martyrs were replenished "by a continuous chain of massacres."[8]

To the north of Armenia is the modern country of Georgia, which was also converted to Christianity in the fourth century in a pyramidal fashion. King Mirian officially adopted Christianity after his wife Nana was healed by a pious Christian woman named Nino, and the king soon mandated that his citizens become baptized. Christianity became the state religion of the kingdom, the Georgian script was created by Christians, and the Bible was translated into that language.

Like Israel, Armenia's strategic location along the continents of Asia, Europe, and Africa made it an easy target for repeated invasions among people groups in the west, east, and south. The Romans and Parthians, long-time political rivals and the powerhouses of the ancient world, menaced the Armenians, who had descended from Indo-European peoples that settled into the region in the seventh century BC. Though speculative, it wouldn't at all be shocking if Christianity had passed through the border of Armenia as early as the first century. According to the *Acts of Addai*, that's exactly what happened. This book claims that Thaddeus (Addai in Aramaic and Syriac), who was one of Jesus's seventy disciples, evangelized the Armenian people from 43 to 66 AD and became patriarch (what is otherwise called a bishop) of the newly established church. Bartholomew, one of Jesus's twelve disciples, reportedly joined Patriarch Thaddeus in 60, whom the locals martyred eight years later, the same year of St. Mark's martyrdom in Alexandria, Egypt.[9]

These claims notwithstanding, more historically plausible evidence for the establishment of Armenian Christianity involves the interrelated, if not partially apocryphal, stories of King Tiridates III (also known as Trdat) and St. Grigor Lusavorich, traditionally known as Gregory the Illuminator. With the support of the Christian-persecuting Emperor Diocletian, Tiridates III became king of Armenia in the 280s or 290s and thus a client of Rome.[10] According to tradition, the Armenians had sent the young prince Tiridates III to Rome after a Parthian nobleman and spy named Anak, the father of Gregory, assassinated Tiridates III's father, King Khosrov II, in Armenia around the year 252.[11] Loyal to Rome for his education and upbringing and opposed to the Parthians due to their treachery, Tiridates III conspired with the Romans against the Parthians by successfully removing the latter from his native country.

Although he originally followed the anti-Christian policies of Emperor Diocletian, Tiridates III had a dramatic conversion experience in the year 301 (or possibly 314) rivaling that of Saint Paul or, at least, Shia LaBeouf. According to accounts, Gregory, who had received a thoroughly Christian education in Cappadocia (in central Turkey), healed the king from demonic possession, thereby proving Christianity to be the true religion of the world. There's an early tradition that Gregory had previously returned to Armenia from Cappadocia as a Christian evangelist and that the king had imprisoned Gregory for his father's crime and for refusing to sacrifice to the goddess Anahit during a religious festival.[12] Gregory reportedly languished in prison for more than a dozen years like a heap of rubbish until officials called him out of the dungeons to cure Tiridates III's sickness. Immediately thereafter the newly cured king ordered the establishment of Christianity throughout Armenia, forever forging the identity of the nation with the Christian religion. Gregory baptized the king and, in conformity with the times, all of the

Etchmiadzin Cathedral in Armenia. Courtesy of Spasavor.

king's subjects likewise received baptism and adopted Christianity as its religion. As was so often the case in the ancient world, the major proof of Christianity's truth was its ability to heal and perform miracles.[13] This is what won the day in Armenia.

The king sent Gregory to Caesarea in Cappadocia for Metropolitan Leontius to ordain him as the catholicos, or leading ecclesiastical bishop, of the Armenian Apostolic Church. Gregory the Illuminator spent the rest of his life on a religious campaign. Under the full force of the law and with the support of the military, he destroyed pagan shrines and uprooted the centuries-long pagan religious heritage of Armenia. Agreeing with the late Nelson Mandela that education is the most powerful weapon to change the world, Gregory educated children of the upper classes and financed the establishment of Christian churches. Mirroring the succession of religious rulers in Armenia, Gregory established a hereditary catholicosate, ensuring the religious stability of the nation. His (male) descendants occupied the leading ecclesiastical chair for generations, and his great-grandson, Sahak, was a highly important bishop who established the Armenian liturgy and worked with local scholars to translate the Bible into the recently created Armenian script. Amazingly, one historian explains, in only a century's time "an indigenous Armenian Christian literature developed that enshrined the faith and deeds of Armenians"[14] together, binding Armenian culture with the Christian religion like cement powder with water.

THE GLORY OF ETHIOPIA

Of course, the same could also be said for Ethiopia, a nation thousands of miles removed from Armenia but similar in many other ways. Like Armenia, Ethiopia is rich in ancient myth, and it's not always possible to separate fact from fiction. According to the national epic of Ethiopia, *The Glory of the Kings*, the queen of Sheba was seduced by the Bible's most barefaced polygamist: King Solomon of Israel. Solomon, a man reported to be "wiser than anyone else" (1 Kings 4:31) yet curiously possessing "700 wives and 300 concubines" (11:3), made the queen of Sheba his object of affection, tricking her to have sex with him while she was visiting the Holy Land. Their offspring, Menelik I, established a dynastic line that sat on the Ethiopian throne until the twentieth century. In the playful literary account of *The Glory of the Kings*, the wisdom of Solomon was only surpassed by the trickery of Menelik. A chip off the old block, Solomon's son swindled the precious Ark of the Covenant out of his father's possession. Even to this day, this ark reportedly resides in a church in the historic capital of Ethiopia, Aksum, guarded around the clock by a consecrated Christian monk lest the calamitous chest should turn up in public and melt the faces of sacrilegious spectators like something out of *Raiders of the Lost Ark*. Despite our burning desire to see the lost ark, we are all in this monk's debt for not having our faces melt like grilled cheese sandwiches.

The historic connection between biblical faith and Ethiopian history extends to the New Testament itself. The book of Acts reports that "an Ethiopian eunuch, an important official in charge of all the treasury of the Kandake (which means 'queen of the Ethiopians')" (8:27), was converted to Christianity by the evangelist Philip in the third decade of the first century. According to the *Apocryphal Acts of the Apostles*, this "important official" returned to his homeland and was joined by the apostle Matthew, who soon launched an evangelistic campaign that would have made Billy Graham blush. Matthew's religious rally was only cut short by the king's brother, who executed the apostle for failing to approve of the king's brother's marriage to his niece. Although this is a charming tradition, it probably never happened. Rival stories placing Matthew in Syria seem more probable than his mass evangelism and martyrdom in Ethiopia. Besides, the term *Ethiopian* in the ancient world was about as vague as the term *Southerner* is in the United States.

> Though not well known, the Nubians of modern-day Sudan and South Sudan (in the kingdom of Cush in the Old Testament) adopted Christianity before many nations in Europe. It was the state religion of all the various Nubian kingdoms by at least the 500s.

Just as the term *Southerner* could refer to just about anyone in America living below the Mason-Dixon Line, so *Ethiopian* was a catchall term referring to anyone living below Egypt, the border of civilized antiquity. If anything, the story of the "Ethiopian eunuch" in the book of Acts alludes to an official in the Nubian or Cushite (Meroitic) kingdom in Sudan, not to a castrated male in the Aksumite kingdom of what we today call Ethiopia.

Whatever we make of the legendary origins of the Christian faith south of Egypt, it was not until around the year 400 that our most credible account of the conversion of Ethiopia to Christianity emerges. According to Rufinus, an eminent Latin-speaking church scholar who was a contemporary and fair-weather friend to Jerome, two Christian schoolboys from modern-day Libya were taken prisoner as slaves in what is today Eritrea and delivered to the king of the Aksumites in Ethiopia in the early 300s. Like Joseph and Daniel in the Old Testament, these two foreign-born boys distinguished themselves among the royal court and became administrators to the king himself—the older brother named Frumentius was the king's treasurer while his younger brother Aedesius was named cupbearer.

Over time these fair-skinned schoolboys gained access to more levers of power. They were instrumental in laying the foundations of Christianity among the royal court of Ethiopia. Frumentius became bishop to the Ethiopians in the first part of the fourth century, being called by those to whom he ministered Abuna Salama, Kassate Berhan—"Father of Peace, Revealer of Light."[15] Meanwhile, Frumentius was reportedly consecrated bishop by Athanasius himself, the feisty and five-time exiled bishop of Alexandria in Egypt who initiated a close relationship between the Egyptian Christians (called Copts) and the Ethiopians for centuries to come. Returning to Ethiopia, Bishop Frumentius baptized King Ezana and the rest of the royal court, as well as converting barbarians and base slaves alike through his supernatural powers and state-backed authority. Later in the fifth century, Frumentius's early efforts at Christianization were strengthened by the arrival of nine Syrian monks, who established monasticism and finished translating the Bible and other religious documents into Ge'ez, the language of the people.

> Begun in the fourth century, the Bible of the Ethiopian Orthodox Church, in Ge'ez, contains the largest canon in the Christian church—81 books. This number includes all the books of the Old Testament excluding Lamentations; the apocryphal or deuterocanonical books; the entire New Testament canon; and additional books such as the *Book of Enoch* and *Jubilees*.

Christianity was solidly in place as the religion of the royal court of Ethiopia by this time. There are, in fact, multiple forms of material evidence attesting to the Christianization of the Aksumite kingdom, illustrating that Ethiopia was one of the first nations on earth to make use of the Christian cross on its currency. As early as the reign of King Ezana, in the first half of the fourth century, coins with an image of the cross boldly proclaimed: "May this [the cross] please the country." Whether it pleased the country or not, Christian artifacts dotted the Ethiopian countryside. An inscription located among one of Ezana's palaces in the capital of Aksum declared:

> In the faith of God, and the power of the Father and Son and Holy Spirit, who saved for me the kingdom by the faith of his son Jesus Christ…I, Ezana, king of the Axumites…give thanks to the Lord my God and I cannot state fully his favors…because he has guided me and I believe in him.[16]

This is an awe-inspiring inscription, but it could have been written in red. For Ezana, like all ancient rulers, was as ruthless as he was religious. His empire, despite the addition of the cross, lived or died by the sword, and neither Ezana nor his empire was inclined to put that relic of steel, as Jesus once commanded, "back in its sheath" (Matt. 26:52). Like Armenia, Georgia, Rome, and many other places in the ancient world, Christianity became the law of the land in Ethiopia through deep faith and brute force.

WRITING ITS OWN SCRIPT

Well before people in Poland or Russia or Sweden had ever beheld a crucifix or set eyes on a provincial church or a magnificent cathedral, let alone had been converted to the faith, the kingdoms in Armenia, Georgia, and Ethiopia had been waving a Christian flag for half a millennium. Truth is, ancient Christianity didn't follow a set script. While the sun of the Christian story in the book of Acts set in Rome—the center of gravity of Western antiquity—it dawned in the orient, and shone over nations from as far away as Afghanistan, India, Iran, and Saudi Arabia. Christianity's presence in the Persian Empire, in fact, became so extensive during the Middle Ages that the leading bishop there came to have oversight over more Christians than any other bishop on planet Earth.

In hindsight, we shouldn't be surprised that Christianity thrived in regions closer to the Euphrates River than the Tiber, closer to Baghdad than to Rome. As a religion birthed right slap in the middle of an ancient highway linking three continents like a cruciform roadmap, it's no coincidence that Christianity traveled just as far north, south, and east as it did west. Indeed, evidence of Christianity's religious road trips across desert villages, exotic marketplaces, and bygone backstreets is well attested in the ancient literature, though, to the chagrin of many a historian, it's virtually impossible to peel away fact from fiction. What we do know, however, is that Christianity was not at all as idealized as we, or even the earliest Christians, imagined. It was as human as it was holy. It was as tarnished as it was resplendent. Its miraculous and mass conversion stories aside, Christianity grew the old fashioned way: by sheer force of will. Not at all discounting the divine aid of the Almighty, Christians sloshed through the mire of ancient societies, converting sin-sodden creatures by any means available: through networks of friendships, through one-on-one evangelism, through displays of grandeur, through intimidation, and through the social pyramid of life. What emerged from the church of yesterday was exactly what emerges from that of today, no more but certainly no less: jars of clay as weak as they are wonderful.

ENDNOTES

1 Rodney Stark, *The Rise of Christianity: How the Obscure, Marginal Jesus Movement Became the Dominant Religious Force in the Western World in a Few Centuries* (Princeton, NJ: Princeton University Press, 1996), 6.

2 According to Theophilus, the seventh bishop of Antioch, "we are called *Christians* on this account, because we are anointed with the oil of God" (*To Autolycus* 1.12).

3 This story comes from the "Acts of Thomas 1-15," in *The Acts of Thomas: Introduction, Text, and Commentary*, 2nd ed., ed. Albertus Klijn and Johannes Frederik (Leiden and Boston: Brill, 2003), 28, 42, 43, 52, 53, 57, 61.

4 Samuel Moffett, *A History of Christianity in Asia*, vol. 1, *Beginnings to 1500* (Maryknoll, NY: Orbis, 1998), 25.

5 Atiya, *History of Eastern Christianity* (Notre Dame, IN: University of Notre Dame Press, 1968), 305.

6 See the recent poll that the Pew Forum conducted at pewforum.org. The poll concluded that 78% of Americans identified as Christians while 98% of Armenians identified as such.

7 Sozomen, *Ecclesiastical History* 2.8

8 Atiya, *History of Eastern Christianity*, 305.

9 Atiya, *History of Eastern Christianity,* 315.

10 Vrej Nerses Nersessian, "Armenian Christianity," in *The Blackwell Companion to Eastern Christianity*, 23–24, for the possibilities of dates.

11 Arra Avakian and Ara John Movsesian, *Armenia: A Journey through History* (Fresno, CA: Electric Press, 2008), 101.

12 Avakian and Movsesian, *Armenia*, 102.

13 For various examples of healing, see the fifth-century Agathangelos, *History of the Armenians*, trans. Robert Thomson (Albany, NY: The State University of New York Press, 1976).

14 Christopher Haas, "The Caucasus," in *Early Christianity in Contexts: An Exploration across Cultures and Continents*, ed. William Tabbernee (Grand Rapids, MI: Baker Academic, 2014), 139.

15 Ephraim Isaac, *The Ethiopian Orthodox Täwahïdo Church* (Trenton, NJ: The Red Sea Press, 2013), 18.

16 Malcolm Choat et al, "The World of the Nile," in *Early Christianity in Context*, 211, 213.

17 "Didascalia Apostolorum," in *Ancient Syriac Documents*, trans. W. Cureton (London: Williams & Norgate, 1864), 33.

Conclusion

THE IRON AND RUST AGE OF CHRISTIANITY

Squinting their eyes into the fog of human origins, the ancient Greeks imagined five ages of humanity. There was the golden age, the silver, the bronze, the heroic, and the iron. According to the Greeks, the current office-holders of humanity, *homo sapiens*, toil in misery during what is decidedly the worst of all eras—the iron age. In this way, the Greeks subscribed to a rather bleak view of humanity, relegating every subsequent era since the golden age as worse than the one before.

Modern Christians have not diverged from this faulty line of thinking. When looking back into the recesses of the Christian past, we get a twinkling in our eyes and a fuzzy feeling in our guts. We fawn over early Christians like roadies at a rock concert. We fantasize that they, particularly those of the biblical variety, always worked peaceably through their differences, always gave their leftovers to the poor, and always paid their electric bills on time.

Despite our best intentions, the first generation of Christians were neither better nor worse than subsequent ones. As we have consistently seen in this honest history of early Christianity, there were no glory days of the church. What has romantically been labeled Christianity's "golden age" had more in common with bronze or iron than gold or silver. Better yet, we could label this time period what the Roman writer Dio Cassius called his age in the late second century: "a kingdom… of iron and rust."[1] "The iron and rust age of the church"—yes, that is a fairer, yet less felicitous, way to describe the trailblazing years of the Christian faith.

This is not by any means to tarnish the heritage of the church—only to situate it within the light of truth. The earliest Christians, we may confidently declare, were not statues of pure gold shining sin-free amid a woeful world. Instead, they were alloyed bodies of believers: mixtures of good and evil, light and dark, Spirit and flesh. As sinful saints, they were just like you and me—real people with real problems living in the real world. This notion not only applies to the Tom, Dick, and Harry's of early Christianity but also to the Peter, Paul, and Mary's. In fact, it applies to all Christians: past, present, and future.

OVERCOMING TEMPTATION

New Testament scholar N. T. Wright once wrote that a constant temptation facing readers of the Gospels is to fashion Jesus in our own image.[2] This helps us understand why radicals always seem to reconstruct a revolutionary Messiah, pacifists a nonviolent Savior, and academics a scholarly Rabbi. Many of us read the pages of Scripture as if they were mere reflections of ourselves. Evangelical Protestants are just as susceptible to this temptation as any other tradition. In fact, one of the many reasons why Christians must study history is because it provides checks and balances to our limited, biased, and even warped senses of reality.

The bent of many believers is also to spare the first generation of Christians from what it means to be a human person: to be clean *and* dirty. Like intellectual laundromats, we wash, disinfect, and bleach images of the earliest Christians, pretending that they all sparkled, shined, and shimmered in body, soul, and mind. Martin Luther, the Protestant reformer of the sixteenth century, coined a Latin phrase to counteract this common Christian belief that a person's justification through Christ entirely rooted out the inclination to sin: *simul iustus et peccator*—"at the same time righteous and sinner." Though declared righteous by God on account of the merits of Christ, people are still people—and people sin. Despite our best efforts to sweep away sin with broomsticks of Bible reading, individual prayer, and sheer will power, there will always be a speck of selfishness, lust, or pride lurking in the corner. No one human, save Jesus, was ever able to rise above the flesh that so weighs down the rest of us. This means, of course, that neither the disciples nor any other believers that followed them offers a fault-free or sin-exempt portrait of Christian living. They weren't supposed to.

Still, old habits die hard. One of the reasons this book has been so challenging to read is because it exposes the enculturated tendency of so many kindhearted believers to uncritically view the earliest Christians as superheroes more so than sin-streaked humans. Fortunately, there is a remedy. Though subtle in some parts, this book has sought to cure common Christian misperceptions of the ancient church by providing accurate information about our history, by questioning our perceived need for early Christianity to be perfect, and by querying what would happen if we actually acknowledged our sordid past. Problem is, of course, it's very hard to heal a congenital illness. And when exploring treatment options, we encounter three common, tenacious symptoms: ignorance, nostalgia, and fear.

Let's go ahead and state the obvious first: Most Christians know next to nothing about church history. When on a rare occasion we try to make a withdrawal from our memory banks of the Christian past, we realize how little money resides in our account. Our bank teller kindly informs us that unless we make a deposit soon, we are in jeopardy of having our account closed for good. Other than Francis of Assisi, Martin Luther, or Mother Teresa, many of us probably cannot name half a dozen characters from the close of the Bible to the dawn of the modern age.

This is not completely our fault. The staple of most Protestants' diet is Bible preaching on Sunday morning. And, yet, of the countless sermons I have listened to over the decades, I can count on my hand the number of times a preacher substantially engaged the church's post-biblical past. And there are few churches that offer Sunday school classes dedicated to any of the persons, literature, topics, times, or insights of Christians who lived after the apostles and before C. S. Lewis.

As Protestants, we are accustomed to looking down upon church history and tradition as distractions from the main event: Scripture. We are interested in the Bible alone, regardless of the fact that the Bible exists for us today because it was sanctioned, consolidated, and preserved by Christians living generations after it was written. It was subsequent Christians who codified our most cherished beliefs, safeguarded them against heretics, and ensured that there actually was a Bible to read once we Protestants arrived on the scene centuries later. Although our sermons are inundated with characters from the biblical past, and inevitably sprinkled with stories of celebrities from the present, we hardly ever hear of how Tertullian interpreted that biblical story, how Ignatius applied that biblical principle, or how Athanasius understood that biblical teaching. We hardly ever hear of how Christians died to keep the Bible from being destroyed, how Christians painstakingly copied by hand every Bible that ever existed for the first 1,500 years of our history, and how the same church that copied this Bible believed it should be understood. In short, we sanitize the lives of the first Christians because we are simply unfamiliar with their stories.

Another reason we disinfect early Christian history is because of our fondness for nostalgia. Nostalgia itself is a billion-dollar industry, urging young adults to watch television shows they viewed as children, prompting middle-aged parents to force their kids into playing sports they did in high school, and compelling seniors to purchase old cars they daydreamed about as teenagers. Fact is, remembering the past is a biblical concept, but nostalgia for it is not. What's more, as much as we try, time does not move backward, we cannot recreate what already happened, and the past was never as perfect as we imagined. While we binge-watch our favorite childhood television shows, we see how corny and clichéd they really were; while forcing our kids to play the sports we once played, we remember the injuries we constantly sustained and how little time we had for other things; and when purchasing refurbished cars, we tire of manually rolling down the windows and only having four radio channels to listen to. When it comes to the first generation of Christians, our idealization of their lives due to nostalgia blinds us to the fact that they were just as spiritually shattered as the rest of us.

Finally, I believe that we exempt the earliest Christians from detailed scrutiny because we fear what will happen if we examine them too closely. As N. T. Wright puts it, "Christianity is afraid of history, frightened that if we really found out what happened in the first century our faith will collapse."[3] What if we were to admit in a moment of brutal self-honesty that the apostle Paul was a broken, contentious, and insecure man who was hard to get along with? Would such human limitations invalidate the truth of his teaching? What if we concluded that Paul's "sharp disagreement" with Barnabas (Acts 15:39), his fierce and public debate with the apostle Peter (Gal. 2:11–21), and the revolving door of friends who eventually "deserted" him such as Phygelus, Hermogenes, and Demas (2 Tim. 1:15, 4:10) was the result of a character flaw (2 Cor. 12:10)?

Paul, the author of nearly half of the books of the New Testament, might be regarded as the greatest saint on earth if it had not been for the fact that we have divinely inspired records detailing just how often he clashed with other Christians and lashed out in red-hot rhetoric against them. But what else should we expect from a self-proclaimed persecutor of the church before his conversion to the gospel (Acts 8:1–3) as well as self-avowed "chief of sinners" afterward (1 Tim. 1:15)? Closer to home, what would happen if we acknowledged that our cherished leaders of today are also broken? What if we recognized that many of them are suffering from depression, are afflicted with loneliness, and are debilitated by stress? Pastors today routinely feel unable to bear the mantle of perfection foisted on them by others who are misinformed about the nature of the Christian life. What if we could release our leaders from the yoke of our misguided understandings of what it means to be a Christian?

Law and Gospel / Damnation and Salvation
by Lucas Cranach the Elder.

LOGIC OF FAITH

To whitewash the early Christian past is to make a huge mistake with lasting consequences. It is to distort the nature of the Christian faith. It is to defy the reason for Christ's incarnation. It is to expect more from believers than is humanly possible. And it is to make us unable to relate to the world. Although the earliest Christians were certainly no animals, neither were they angels. They were broken humans in the process of being redeemed by a faultless Redeemer. They were leaders who limped, martyrs who wavered, churchgoers who offered curious worship, apologists who overreached, theologians who demonized diversity, believers who wanted more than the Bible contained, aristocrats who overstepped their bounds, men who denigrated sex, and missionaries who employed questionable evangelistic techniques.

Rather than invalidating the Christian faith, however, their lives—warts and all—authenticated it. For the more we see the foibles, mishaps, and gaffes of Paul, Ignatius, and Augustine, the more we see the flawlessness of Christ. The more we see the failures of our greatest leaders, the more we see the glories of our sinless Savior. And the more we see the clear limitations of the human condition, the more we the strengths of the risen Lord. "It is not the healthy who need a doctor," Jesus famously declared, "but the sick" (Mark 2:17). The history of the church is not a fabled account of angels masquerading as humans; it is a beautiful love story of how a Great Physician died while saving patients intent on killing him. We naturally expect to see those who were saved to live a life of thankfulness to the physician who healed them, but we can hardly expect them to be perfect patients who suffered without a word of complaint, who never doubted the treatment of the medical staff, and who showed no sign of relapse.

ENDNOTES

1 Dio Cassius, *Roman History*, vol. 8, *Books 71-80*, Loeb Classical Library, no. 177, trans. Earnest Cary, (Cambridge, MA: Harvard University Press, 1982), 69.

2 N. T. Wright, *The New Testament and the People of God*, vol. 1, *Christian Origins and the Question of God* (Minneapolis, MN: Fortress Press, 1992), 10.

3 Wright, *The New Testament and the People of God*, 10.

INDEX